# Understanding Philosophy of Religion

# Edexcel Teacher's Book

Libby Ahluwalia

Folens

United Kingdom: Folens Publishers, Waterslade House, Thame Road, Haddenham, Buckinghamshire HP17 8NT. email: folens@folens.com

Ireland: Folens Publishers, Greenhills Road, Tallaght, Dublin 24. email: info@folens.ie



Editors: Jenny Roberts and Jane Bishop

Page design and layout: Clifford Hayes, Hayes Design

Cover design: Clifford Hayes, Hayes Design

Cover image: Death Valley dunes © iStock

First published 2008 by Folens Limited

Every effort has been made to contact copyright holders of material used in this publication. If any copyright holder has been overlooked, we should be pleased to make the necessary arrangements.

British Library Cataloguing in Publication Data. A catalogue record for this publication is available from the British Library.

ISBN 978-1-85008-273-6

**Acknowledgements**

The authors and publishers wish to thank the following for permission to use copyright material: pp 82–3 – Free Inquiry for an extract from Peter Atkins, 'Awesome vs. Adipose: Who *Really* Works Hardest to Banish Ignorance?' *Free Inquiry* (Spring 1998) 18:2. Copyright © 1998 Council for Secular Humanism; pp. 119–20 – Guardian News & Media Ltd for Mark Vernon, 'Face to faith: God is only apprehended when words at last fall silent', *The Guardian*, 25.11.06. Copyright © Guardian News & Media Ltd 2006; pp. 85–6 – Charlie Liebert for an extract from www.sixdaycreation.com; p. 93 – The Monist for an extract from David and Marjorie Haight 'An ontological argument for the Devil' in *The Monist* (1970) 54:2. Copyright © 1970 The Monist: An International Quarterly Journal of General Philosophical Inquiry, Peru, Illinois, 61354; p. 102 – New Humanist Magazine for an extract from Laurie Taylor interview, *New Humanist* (October 2004) 119:5; p. 99 – Sigmund Freud Copyrights by arrangement with Paterson Marsh Ltd. for an extract from Sigmund Freud, *The Future of an Illusion*, first published 1927, from *The Standard Edition of the Complete Psychological Works of Sigmund Freud*, The Hogarth Press (1961), Vol. 21 pp. 16-18; p. 101 – Taylor & Francis Books UK for an extract from Bertrand Russell, *Why I am not a Christian*, Routledge (2004). Copyright © The Bertrand Russell Peace Foundation Ltd. and Taylor & Francis.

# Contents

# Introduction

## About this resource book

This book is designed to provide teachers and students with extra source material and lesson ideas to support teaching in Religious Studies. It is a useful bank of material to supplement classroom teaching; it is not necessary to work slavishly through every page.

## Activity/research pages

Some pages are designed as worksheets for students to use either in the classroom or for homework tasks. Several of them invite the students to familiarise themselves with biblical material, in recognition that many will be studying the Philosophy of Religion from a mainly Christian perspective. This is partly to address complaints from schools and universities that students of Religious Studies often lack an understanding of the biblical background to religious ideas, and partly because it is difficult for students to comment on Christian ideas unless they are familiar with them.

The discussion pages are designed so that they can be reproduced for the students as handouts if desired. Some of these will work well as starter activities, as a way of introducing the topic, while others might be more appropriate to tackle once the students are familiar with the material, and some are designed to stretch and challenge the most able. Some pages can be used as whole-class activities, as work to set when the teacher needs to be absent, or as homework tasks to help pupils engage with the topics.

## Revision test questions

Some sections have short-answer questions relating to the content of the unit – some of the questions are easier than others. These can be used in a variety of ways.

They could be used as straightforward class tests at the end of each unit of study, to keep track of progress and encourage pupils to learn material as they study the course.

Alternatively, the questions could be used as the basis for revision games, which can be a good way of lightening the pressure as examinations loom and taking some of the drudgery out of revision, as well as a way of encouraging more reticent members of the class to take part:

- the class could be divided into teams, or students could compete individually, with the questions being asked alternately or on a 'first on the buzzer' basis;
- games could be set up using the rules of television quiz shows such as '*Fifteen to One*', '*The Weakest Link*' or '*Mastermind*';
- the questions could be used with board games such as 'Trivial Pursuit', or they could becombined with a basic board such as Snakes and Ladders, where a throw of the dice and a chance to move forward depends on a correct answer to a question;
- the questions can be used as in children's party games such as Pass the Parcel, where a student gets a question whenever the music stops and earns a sweet for answering correctly (these games seem to be particularly popular);
- the students will probably think of their own ideas too.

## 'Key point' and key vocabulary revision summary pages

The revision summary pages can be copied for the students to keep in their files, or used as examples from which the students make their own revision notes.

## Practice essay questions and marking schemes

There are practice essay questions and suggested marking schemes. The questions could be used as practice homework tasks for the students during the course, or as mock examination questions for writing under timed conditions.

## Assessment for learning exercises

The assessment for learning exercises present students with some examples of answers to exam questions. These are **not meant as model answers.** As an exercise, students consider the pieces of work and measure them against the levels of response provided by Edexcel. They consider the strengths and weaknesses of the sample answers, and decide which mark-band would be appropriate. The students can then apply the same skills of assessment to their own work and to each other's.

# Guide to marking AS essays

## Go to INSET:

If at all possible, attend the INSET courses offered by Edexcel, where you will have the chance to reflect on last year's examinations, see sample scripts and learn how marks were awarded. Better still, apply to become an examiner. When you are faced with all the marking to do, you will curse the day you ever agreed to take it on, but afterwards you will recognise that it is by far the best way you can learn about how to help your own students to succeed.

## Judging AS standard:

Obviously, decisions about whether a piece of work is good or bad depends on reasonable expectations of the student. When marking AS work, the idea is that full marks should be given if the work is the absolute best that could reasonably be expected of a 17 year old who has been studying the subject for one year. (Expectations should also be adjusted depending on whether the work has been written under exam conditions, or at leisure with notes.) Some teachers try to measure the work against what they imagine they would have written themselves as a mature adult with postgraduate level qualifications, but this is not fair. Each piece of work should be marked with AS in mind, and compared with the levels of response. Try not to measure the students in the group against each other – if there is an outstanding pupil working well above AS level, this does not mean that the others should lose marks. It is unlikely that the full range of ability will be represented in one group, so if everyone deserves high (or low) marks then give them.

## Positive awarding:

The principle of positive awarding means that when marking a piece of work, you look for opportunities to give credit, rather than to penalise. Rather than thinking of the things that you would have included but the student has left out, look for what has been included and aim to reward it. Don't take marks off for anything – if there is a statement or even a whole passage that is inaccurate or irrelevant, ignore it (although you can of course write comments!).

## Levels of response:

The examiners mark the work according to levels of response. There are different levels for each assessment objective, and students will not necessarily be in the same level for different skills. The principle is that the marker looks for the level description which is the 'best fit' for the student's work. The work might not display all the characteristics described, but it will probably be clear which level best fits the work. Then the marker has to decide whereabouts within that level is the right mark to award. If there is doubt between two marks, in the spirit of positive awarding go for the higher mark.

# Stocking your library

This list is not 'the official Edexcel list of set texts'. You may well have found other books, not on this list, which you and your students enjoy using. However, some teachers are daunted by the task of choosing how to spend a limited book budget. The books on this list are those that I particularly like and that my own students find helpful. There are plenty of other good books available too.

✓ Peter Cole, *Philosophy of Religion* (Hodder Murray, 2004)

✓ Peter Cole, *Religious Experience* (Hodder Murray, 2005)

✓ Brian Davies, *An Introduction to the Philosophy of Religion* (Oxford University Press, 2003)

✓ C. Stephen Evans, *Philosophy of Religion: Thinking about Faith* (InterVarsity Press, 2001)

✓ John Hick (ed.), *Classical and Contemporary Readings in the Philosophy of Religion* (Prentice Hall, 1991)

✓ John Hick, *Philosophy of Religion* (Prentice Hall, 1989)

✓ Bryan Magee, *The Story of Philosophy* (Dorling Kindersley, 1998)

✓ Michael Palmer, *The Question of God* (Routledge, 2001)

✓ Daniel L. Pals, *Seven Theories of Religion* (Oxford University Press, 1996)

✓ John Polkinghorne, *Belief in God in an Age of Science* (Yale University Press 2003)

✓ Richard Swinburne, *Is There a God?* (Oxford University Press, 1996)

✓ Richard Swinburne, *The Existence of God* (Clarendon Press, 2004)

✓ Mel Thompson, *Science and Religion* (Hodder Murray, 2000)

✓ Peter Vardy, *The Puzzle of God* (Fount, 1999)

# What is religion?

**Which of the following do you think can be classified as 'religion'? Try to say why you think it meets the definition 'religion', or why it doesn't. Which factors are significant, and which are irrelevant?**

- Being a fanatical Arsenal supporter – spending significant amounts of money on season tickets; travelling sometimes long distances to matches; meeting with other Arsenal supporters to watch matches on television; wearing the kit; talking about Arsenal to anyone who will listen, and drinking out of an Arsenal mug.

- Being a Buddhist – believing that there is no God; believing that people do not have souls; visiting the Buddhist temple to meditate in solitude; reading Buddhist literature, especially sacred writings; being a vegetarian; trying to follow the Noble Eightfold Path in daily life; talking about Buddhist beliefs to friends and colleagues.

- Being an active member of the Communist party – believing that there is no God; devoting time to Communist causes such as the production and selling of political literature; studying Communism and the writings of other Communists; meeting regularly with other Communists to discuss future plans; understanding the society in which you live with a Communist perspective; making ethical decisions based on Communist principles.

- Being Jewish – having a Jewish mother; keeping a kosher kitchen; going to synagogue every Saturday; believing in one God; following the rules of the Jewish scriptures; choosing to marry a fellow Jew; praying regularly; celebrating all the Jewish festivals and observing Yom Kippur.

# Assessing the strength of inductive arguments

**Many Design arguments for the existence of God are examples of inductive arguments using analogy. Here are some other examples of inductive arguments using analogy. Decide whether they are persuasive arguments – what are their strengths and/or weaknesses?**

1.
Lettuces, grass, oak trees, willows and my handbag are all green.
Lettuce, grass, oak trees and willows all require water, sun and carbon dioxide to stay green.
Therefore, my handbag needs water, sun and carbon dioxide to stay green.

2.
Many cigarette smokers need hospital treatment for problems they would never have had if they didn't smoke.
Many sports enthusiasts also need hospital treatment for problems they would never have had if they didn't play sport.
If smokers should have to pay extra tax on cigarettes as a contribution to the health service, then sports players should have to pay extra tax on sports equipment.

3.
My electric kettle, computer and lawnmower all have electric plugs, and only work when I plug them into sockets.
My new iron has an electric plug.
Therefore, the iron will only work when I plug it into a socket.

**You need to think about: how good is the analogy? Are the analogies 'comparing like with like'?**

Look again at this Design argument for the existence of God:

> The universe works according to regular rules and patterns, like a machine.
> Machines which work according to regular rules and patterns are made by intelligent designers.
> Therefore, the universe must have been made by an intelligent designer.

**How good is the analogy? Is the argument persuasive?**

# Design arguments: for discussion

**Pied Beauty**

*GLORY be to God for dapple things,*
*For skies of couple-colour as a brinded cow;*
*For rose-moles all in stipple upon trout that swim;*
*Fresh-firecoal chestnut-falls, finches' wings;*
*Landscape plotted and pieced – fold, fallow and plough;*
*And all trades, their gear and tackle and trim.*

*All things counter, original, spare, strange;*
*Whatever is fickle, freckled (who knows how?)*
*With swift, slow; sweet, sour; adazzle, dim;*
*He fathers-forth whose beauty is past change:*
*Praise him.*

Gerard Manley Hopkins

In this poem, Hopkins praises God for the variety of nature, especially for all speckled and spotted things.

- What aspects of nature do you find particularly beautiful?
- Are there aspects of the natural world that you think are ugly?
- Do you think that beauty is a matter of opinion, or a matter of fact?
- Do you think beauty in nature happens by chance, or was it designed?
- How might (a) F. R. Tennant and (b) Richard Dawkins respond to this poem?
- How do you think Hopkins might respond to J. S. Mill's view that nature is cruel?

# Design arguments: William Paley's watch analogy

In crossing a heath, suppose I pitched my foot against a stone and were asked how the stone came to be there, I might possibly answer that for anything I knew to the contrary it had lain there forever; nor would it, perhaps, be very easy to show the absurdity of this answer. But suppose I had found a watch upon the ground, and it should be inquired how the watch happened to be in that place, I should hardly think of the answer which I had before given, that for anything I knew the watch might have always been there. Yet why should not this answer serve for the watch as well as for the stone; why is it not as admissible in the second case as in the first?

For this reason, and for no other, namely, that when we come to inspect the watch, we perceive – what we could not discover in the stone – that its several parts are framed and put together for a purpose, e.g. that is to say, that they are so formed and adjusted as to produce motion, and that motion so regulated as to point out the hour of the day; that if the different parts had been differently shaped from what they are, or placed after any other manner or in any other order than that in which they are placed, either no motion at all would have been carried on in the machine, or none which would have answered the use that is now served by it. To reckon up a few of the plainest of these parts and of their offices, all tending to one result: we see a cylindrical box containing a coiled elastic spring, which, by its endeavour to relax itself, turns round the box. We next observe a flexible chain – artificially wrought for the sake of flexure – communicating the action of the spring from the box to the fusee.

We then find a series of wheels, the teeth of which catch in and apply to each other, conducting the motion from the fusee to the balance and from the balance to the pointer, and at the same time, by the size and shape of those wheels, so regulating that motion is to terminate in causing an index, by an equable and measured progression, to pass over a given space in a given time. We take notice that the wheels are made of brass, in order to keep them from rust; the springs of steel, no other metal being so elastic; that over the face of the watch there is placed a glass, a material employed in no other part of the work, but in the room of which, if there had been any other than a transparent substance, the hour could not be seen without opening the case.

This mechanism being observed – it requires indeed an examination of the instrument, and perhaps some previous knowledge of the subject, to perceive and understand it; but being once, as we have said, observed and understood – the inference we think is inevitable, that the watch must have had a maker – that there must have existed, at some time and at some place or other, an artificer or artificers who formed it for the purpose which we find it actually to answer, who completely comprehended its construction and designed its use.

(from *Natural Theology* by William Paley)

# Design arguments: Mackie's conclusion

'Whereas Swinburne says that 'the universe might so naturally have been chaotic', it is hard to see how there could be things at all without their having some regular ways of working. No doubt there could have been less regularity and more sheer randomness than there seems to be; but there is no good reason to take one of these to be, in itself and *a priori*, more likely than the other.

'... objections can be avoided only by going back to the supposedly *a priori* principle that a god is self-explanatory, whereas everything else is in need of further explanation.

'... I conclude that the argument for design cannot be revived. The advance of science has destroyed the starting-points which made it initially plausible and attractive in the eighteenth century, while the general philosophical objections which were brought against it even then by Kant and, above all, by Hume, remain in force against Swinburne's restatement of it, and, I surmise against all possible reconstructions.'

(from J. L. Mackie, *The Miracle of Theism*, Oxford University Press, 1982)

## Questions

1. In Mackie's view, Swinburne assumes that the universe would be chaotic unless God ordered it – Mackie questions this assumption. Do you think that the universe would be chaotic if there were no God to organise it? Or is order something which we should expect to see in anything that exists successfully?

2. The principle that God is 'self-explanatory' applies to the cosmological argument as well as to design arguments. Is it reasonable to suggest that God could create the world without being created himself, or does this not make sense?

3. Mackie argues that advances in science since the eighteenth century have undermined design arguments. Which advances in particular might he have in mind? Is he right, in your view, to conclude that they have 'destroyed' the bases of arguments from design?

# Is God's goodness revealed to us in the natural world?

**We plough the fields and scatter**

1.
We plough the fields, and scatter the good seed on the land,
But it is fed and watered by God's almighty hand;
He sends the snow in winter, the warmth to swell the grain,
The breezes and the sunshine, and soft refreshing rain.

*Refrain:*
*All good gifts around us*
*Are sent from heaven above,*
*Then thank the Lord, O thank the Lord*
*For all His love.*

2.
He only is the Maker of all things near and far;
He paints the wayside flower, He lights the evening star;
The winds and waves obey Him, by Him the birds are fed;
Much more to us, His children, He gives our daily bread.

*Refrain*

3.
We thank Thee, then, O Father, for all things bright and good,
The seed time and the harvest, our life, our health,
and our food;
No gifts have we to offer, for all Thy love imparts,
But that which Thou desirest, our humble, thankful hearts.

*Refrain*

(Matthias Claudius, 1782)

In this well-known Christian hymn, God is thanked for his providence.

1. Make a list of the things that this hymn thanks God for providing.

2. The hymn claims that 'All good gifts around us are sent from heaven above. How far would you agree with this point of view?

3. What about the bad things around us, for example those which adversely affect the fruitfulness of the earth – drought, flood, unseasonable frosts, foot and mouth disease, avian flu, coddling moths, slugs? Must these also have been sent from heaven above, if the good gifts are attributed to God? If not, where did they come from – or are there no intrinsically bad things, just our own bad attitudes towards them?

4. How does Genesis 3:17–19 account for the problems encountered by those who grow food for a living? Does such a response adequately address the problems, or does it raise more issues?

# Design arguments: key points revision sheet

- Design arguments are called teleological because they look at the end result (the world). They are inductive, *a posteriori* arguments.

- Design arguments use analogies between the world and manufactured machines.

- The Bible can be read to support design arguments: *'The heavens tell out the glory of God, the vault of heaven reveals his handiwork.'* (Psalm 19).

- Aquinas' Fifth Way is a design argument – nature moves towards its goal because it is guided by God as an archer guides an arrow.

- William Paley used the analogy of finding a watch on a heath to argue that the natural world shows evidence of design, in his book *Natural Theology*. He argued that the more we learn about different animals and plants, the more clearly we can see evidence of intelligent design.

- David Hume said that there could be other explanations for apparent design, for example, a committee of gods; there is no reason to assume the Christian God as a cause. Order will be part of any world, because without it the world would not survive. He thought the analogy between the world and a watch was weak.

- John Stuart Mill said that if nature points to the existence of God, it is a cruel God.

- Darwin suggested natural selection as an alternative explanation for apparent design in the world. This view is supported by Richard Dawkins in *The Blind Watchmaker*.

- F. R. Tennant thought the beauty of the world could not be explained by science. He suggested that the world has been 'fine-tuned' to allow human life to develop (the anthropic principle).

- Richard Swinburne agrees with Paley that there is design in the world which suggests the probable existence of God.

# Design arguments: revision test questions

1. What was the name of the book in which Aquinas set out his Five Ways?

2. Which of the Five Ways is a version of the teleological argument?

3. What was J. S. Mill's major criticism of teleological arguments?

4. Who said '… *the contrivances of nature surpass the contrivances of art, in the complexity, subtility, and curiosity of the mechanism.*'?

5. How did Hume criticise teleological arguments?

6. Why was the work of Darwin seen as undermining teleological arguments?

7. Name a book by Richard Dawkins which challenges arguments from design.

8. What is the main point made by Tennant's aesthetic argument?

9. Name a modern thinker who supports Paley's design argument.

# Design arguments: revision test answers

1. *Summa Theologica*

2. 5

3. That nature is cruel, so the natural world reveals the existence of a cruel God if it reveals God at all.

4. William Paley

5. The analogy with a watch is a bad one; there could be other explanations for design; it does not point to the God of Christianity; any surviving world will appear designed.

6. Because it presented an alternative explanation for apparent design in animals and plants: natural selection.

7. *The Blind Watchmaker*, *The Selfish Gene*, *The God Delusion*, *River out of Eden*

8. Natural explanations cannot account for the beauty of the world.

9. Many: Swinburne or Tennant or accept any other reasonable answer.

# Design arguments: assessment for learning

Have a look at the following piece of writing, and also look at the level descriptors examiners use when they are judging the quality of your work at AS level.

1. What do you think would be the right band for the work, for Assessment Objective (AO) 1?

For AO1, the work should demonstrate knowledge and understanding. You are looking for:

- Relevance to the question (not just relevance to the general topic)
- Accuracy
- Detail
- Appropriate examples and references
- Thoroughness

2. What do you think would be the right band for AO2?

For AO2, the work should show evaluative skill. You are looking for:

- Relevance to the question
- Reference to different points of view
- Clearly explained reasoning
- A clear and well-supported conclusion that answers the question

3. Once you have decided on the sort of mark you think this work should get, write some comments advising the student so that he or she knows how to improve. Make sure you include some positive comments, saying what was good, as well as saying what the student could do better next time.

## Sample student answer

**(a) Explain the main features of design arguments for the existence of God.**

Design arguments for the existence of God are also known as teleological arguments. The word teleological comes from the Greek *telos*, which means tail or end. The most famous design argument comes from a man called William Paley.

One day, Paley was walking along a heath when he found a watch. He looked at the way the watch fitted together, and saw that all the different parts had a job to do and all worked together so that the watch told the time. He said that the world is like a watch. When we look at the world and all the different things in it, we can see that all the animals and plants are carefully made so that they suit their habitats. We can see how the human eye works like a camera, with different parts all suited to perform the function of seeing. Paley concluded that there must be a God who designed the world, just as there must have been a watchmaker who designed the watch.

Other people, however, disagreed with Paley. David Hume, a Scottish philosopher, argued that there could be other explanations for the design of the world. It is as if we are looking at a pair of weighing scales, and we can only see one side. We can see the order in the world, but we don't know what caused it. It might have been a whole committee of Gods, or it might have been a stupid God who only arrived at this world after making lots of mistakes. Mille argued that if design arguments show the existence of a God who made it all, then he must be a cruel God who wants us to be unhappy. Mill said this because in nature, many plants and animals only exist by killing each other, and some of them are designed to kill in a cruel way.

**(b) 'Order in the world could have come about by chance. There is no reason to assume the existence of God to explain it.' To what extent would you agree with this statement?**

Hume said order in the world could have come about by chance. He also said that we can never really know if this world is an ordered world or not, because we have nothing to compare it with. There might be a lot of other worlds out there with more order than our own, and if we could see them, we would realise that this world is disordered. Richard Dawkins also said that the order in the world is the result of chance. In his book 'The Blind Watchmaker', he criticised Paley's conclusions. Dawkins believes that Darwin's theories have successfully shown that the world was not designed by God and that science gives a better explanation.

Other people disagree. Swinburne says that the teleological argument is a good one, and that he agrees with Paley. Aquinas also thought that Paley was right. In his Five Ways, he gave the example of an archer shooting an arrow, to show that everything moves towards its goal because there is a guiding hand behind it.

In conclusion, we can see that there are different opinions about whether the order in the world is brought about by chance.

## Practice exam question

Students' work should be measured against the Edexcel levels of response for AS Religious Studies.

**(a) Examine the main strengths and weaknesses of design arguments for the existence of God.**

**(b) 'The world provides clear evidence of the existence of a loving God.' Discuss.**

**Marking guide:**

AO1

The top-level answer should focus precisely on the question in terms of outlining strengths and weaknesses rather than just describing teleological arguments. For the highest marks, a range of strengths and weaknesses should be given, such as the appeal of the argument to experience of wonder at the beauty of nature as a strength (with reference to Tennant), or the existence of other possible explanations for apparent design in the universe as a weakness (with reference to Hume). A high level answer will recognise that design arguments are inductive, *a posteriori* arguments. Accurate reference will be made to a variety of thinkers, such as Aquinas, Paley, Tennant, Swinburne, Hume, Mill and Dawkins. Their views will not be presented simply as a list, but as part of a clear explanation which directly addresses the question. The student will use a range of key technical terms with accuracy, such as 'teleological', 'purposive', 'analogy' and 'sceptic'.

**(b) 'The world provides clear evidence of the existence of a loving God.' Discuss.**

AO2

To achieve a high level, students should make an attempt at critical analysis. They should make reference to alternative different viewpoints and use balanced reasoning. Their arguments should be expressed accurately and fluently, and they should use a range of technical vocabulary. They should reach a conclusion which is well supported by the rest of the answer, rather than just tacked on at the end. They should be able to sustain a critical analysis and use the thinking of key scholars as well as using specialist terms with accuracy. For this question, students should give an argument which focuses clearly on the issues in the question – whether there is 'clear evidence' (which might be supported by Paley), whether the evidence sways the balance of probability (Swinburne) or whether there is no evidence at all (Dawkins), for example. They should also consider whether it is evidence of a loving God – the views of Mill and Hume would be useful here.

# Cosmological arguments: Richard Taylor

From Richard Taylor *Metaphysics* (Prentice-Hall 1963)

It would seem, then, that the world, in case it happens to exist at all – and this is quite beyond doubt – is contingent and thus dependent upon something other than itself for its existence, if it depends upon anything at all. And it must depend upon something, for otherwise there could be no reason why it exists in the first place. Now that upon which the world depends must be something that either exists by its own nature or does not. If it does not exist by its own nature, then it, in turn, depends for its existence upon something else, and so on. Now then, we can say either of two things; namely (1) that the world depends for its existence upon something else, which in turn depends on still another thing, this depending upon still another, *ad infinitum*; or (2) that the world derives its existence from something that exists by its own nature and which is accordingly eternal and imperishable, and is the creator of heaven and earth. The first of these alternatives, however, is impossible, for it does not render a sufficient reason why anything should exist in the first place. Instead of supplying a reason why any world should exist, it repeatedly begs off giving a reason. It explains what is dependent and perishable in terms of what is itself dependent and perishable, leaving us still without a reason why perishable things should exist at all, which is what we are seeking. Ultimately, then, it would seem that the world, or the totality of contingent or perishable things, in case it exists at all, must depend upon something that is necessary and imperishable, and which accordingly exists, not in dependence upon something else, but by its own nature.

**Questions**

1. Explain what Richard Taylor means when he describes the world as 'contingent'.

2. Find a phrase or sentence in the passage that illustrates the concept of 'infinite regress'.

3. Why does Taylor think that an infinite regress is impossible?

4. Do you think that he is right to suggest there has to be 'sufficient reason' for the world to exist at all?

5. Which of Aquinas' three cosmological arguments does Taylor's passage most resemble?

6. How might Bertrand Russell have responded to this passage (if he were still alive)?

# Cosmological argument: from Hume's *Dialogues Concerning Natural Religion*

**In David Hume's *Dialogues Concerning Natural Religion*, different characters debate some of the arguments for the existence of God. Here, Demea begins by presenting the cosmological argument, and Cleanthes replies with some criticisms.**

Whatever exists must have a cause or reason of its existence; it being absolutely impossible for any thing to produce itself, or be the cause of its own existence. In mounting up, therefore, from effects to causes, we must either go on in tracing an infinite succession, without any ultimate cause at all; or must at last have recourse to some ultimate cause, that is necessarily existent: now, that the first supposition is absurd, may be thus proved. In the infinite chain or succession of causes and effects, each single effect is determined to exist by the power and efficacy of that cause which immediately preceded; but the whole eternal chain or succession, taken together, is not determined or caused by any thing; and yet it is evident that it requires a cause or reason, as much as any particular object which begins to exist in time. The question is still reasonable, why this particular succession of causes existed from eternity, and not any other succession, or no succession at all. If there be no necessarily existent being, any supposition which can be formed is equally possible; nor is there any more absurdity in Nothing's having existed from eternity, than there is in that succession of causes which constitutes the universe. What was it, then, which determined Something to exist rather than Nothing, and bestowed being on a particular possibility, exclusive of the rest? External causes, there are supposed to be none. Chance is a word without a meaning. Was it Nothing? But that can never produce any thing. We must, therefore, have recourse to a necessarily existent Being, who carries the REASON of his existence in himself, and who cannot be supposed not to exist, without an express contradiction. There is, consequently, such a Being; that is, there is a Deity.

I shall not leave it to Philo, said Cleanthes, though I know that the starting objections is his chief delight, to point out the weakness of this metaphysical reasoning. It seems to me so obviously ill-grounded, and at the same time of so little consequence to the cause of true piety and religion, that I shall myself venture to shew the fallacy of it.

I shall begin with observing, that there is an evident absurdity in pretending to demonstrate a matter of fact, or to prove it by any arguments *a priori*. Nothing is demonstrable, unless the contrary implies a contradiction. Nothing, that is distinctly conceivable, implies a contradiction. Whatever we conceive as existent, we can also conceive as non-existent. There is no being, therefore, whose non- existence implies a contradiction. Consequently there is no being, whose existence is demonstrable. I propose this argument as entirely decisive, and am willing to rest the whole controversy upon it.

It is pretended that the Deity is a necessarily existent being; and this necessity of his existence is attempted to be explained by asserting, that if we knew his whole essence or nature, we should perceive it to be as impossible for him not to exist, as for twice two not to be four. But it is evident that this can never happen, while our faculties remain the same as at present. It will still be possible for us, at any time, to conceive the non-existence of what we formerly conceived to exist; nor can the mind ever lie under a necessity of supposing any object to remain always in being; in the same manner as we lie under a necessity of always conceiving twice two to be four. The words, therefore, necessary existence, have no meaning; or, which is the same thing, none that is consistent.

But further, why may not the material universe be the necessarily existent being, according to this pretended explication of necessity? We dare not affirm that we know all the qualities of matter; and for aught we can determine, it may contain some qualities, which, were they known, would make its non-existence appear as great a contradiction as that twice two is five. I find only one argument employed to prove, that the material world is not the necessarily existent Being: and this argument is derived from the contingency both of the matter and the form of the world. "Any particle of matter," it is said, "may be conceived to be annihilated; and any form may be conceived to be altered. Such an annihilation or alteration, therefore, is not impossible." But it seems a great partiality not to perceive, that the same argument extends equally to the Deity, so far as we have any conception of him; and that the mind can at least imagine him to be non-existent, or his attributes to be altered. It must be some unknown, inconceivable qualities, which can make his non-existence appear impossible, or his attributes unalterable: and no reason can be assigned, why these qualities may not belong to matter. As they are altogether unknown and inconceivable, they can never be proved incompatible with it.

Add to this, that in tracing an eternal succession of objects, it seems absurd to enquire for a general cause or first author. How can any thing, that exists from eternity, have a cause, since that relation implies a priority in time, and a beginning of existence?

In such a chain, too, or succession of objects, each part is caused by that which preceded it, and causes that which succeeds it. Where then is the difficulty? But the WHOLE, you say, wants a cause. I answer, that the uniting of these parts into a whole, like the uniting of several distinct countries into one kingdom, or several distinct members into one body, is performed merely by an arbitrary act of the mind, and has no influence on the nature of things. Did I shew you the particular causes of each individual in a collection of twenty particles of matter, I should think it very unreasonable, should you afterwards ask me, what was the cause of the whole twenty. This is sufficiently explained in explaining the cause of the parts.

**Questions**

1. What are the main criticisms Cleanthes makes of Demea's cosmological argument?

2. To what extent are his criticisms valid, in your view?

# Cosmological argument: the debate between Russell and Copleston

**This famous debate between Bertrand Russell and the Jesuit priest and philosopher Fr. Frederick Copleston was first broadcast on BBC radio's Third Programme in 1948. This transcript is taken from *Bertrand Russell On God and Religion*, edited by Al Seckel (Prometheus Books, 1986).**

**C:** As we are going to discuss the existence of God, it might perhaps be as well to come to some provisional agreement as to what we understand by the term "God". I presume that we mean a supreme personal being – distinct from the world and creator of the world. Would you agree – provisionally at least – to accept this statement as the meaning of the term "God"?

**R:** Yes, I accept this definition.

**C:** Well, my position is the affirmative position that such a being actually exists, and that His existence can be proved philosophically. Perhaps you would tell me if your position is that of agnosticism or of atheism. I mean, would you say that the non-existence of God can be proved?

**R:** No, I should not say that: my position is agnostic.

**C:** Would you agree with me that the problem of God is a problem of great importance? For example, would you agree that if God does not exist, human beings and human history can have no other purpose than the purpose they choose to give themselves, which — in practice — is likely to mean the purpose which those impose who have the power to impose it?

**R:** Roughly speaking, yes, though I should have to place some limitation on your last clause.

**C:** Would you agree that if there is no God – no absolute Being – there can be no absolute values? I mean, would you agree that if there is no absolute good that the relativity of values results?

**R:** No, I think these questions are logically distinct. Take, for instance, G. E. Moore's *Principia Ethica*, where he maintains that there is a distinction of good and evil, that both of these are definite concepts. But he does not bring in the idea of God to support that contention.

**C:** Well, suppose we leave the question of good till later, till we come to the moral argument, and I give first a metaphysical argument. I'd like to put the main weight on thc metaphysical argument based on Leibniz's argument from "Contingency" and then later we might discuss the moral argument. Suppose I give a brief statement on the metaphysical argument and then we go on to discuss it?

**R:** That seems to me to be a very good plan.

**C:** Well, for clarity's sake, I'll divide the argument into distinct stages. First of all, I should say, we know that there are at least some beings in the world which do not contain in themselves the reason for their existence. For example, I depend on my parents, and now on the air, and on food, and so on. Now, secondly, the world is simply the real or imagined totality or aggregate of individual objects, none of which contain in themselves alone the reason for their existence. There isn't any world distinct from the objects which form it, any more than the human race is something apart from the members. Therefore, I should say, since objects or events exist, and since no object of experience contains within itself reason of its existence, this reason, the totality of objects, must have a reason external to itself. That reason must be an existent being. Well, this being is either itself the reason for its own existence, or it is not. If it is, well and good. If it is not, then we must proceed farther. But if we proceed to infinity in that sense, then there's no explanation of existence at all. So, I should say, in order to explain existence, we must come to a being which contains within itself the reason for its own existence, that is to say, which cannot not exist.

**R:** This raises a great many points and it is not altogether easy to know where to begin, but I think that, perhaps, in answering your argument, the best point at which to begin is the question of necessary being. The word "necessary," I should maintain, can only be applied significantly to propositions. And, in fact, only to such as are analytic — that is to say — such as it is self-contradictory to deny. I could only admit a necessary being if there were a being whose existence it is self-contradictory to deny. I should like to know whether you would accept Leibniz's division of propositions into truths of reason and truths of fact. The former — the truths of reason — being necessary.

**C:** Well, I certainly should not subscribe to what seems to be Leibniz's idea of truths of reason and truths of fact, since it would appear that, for him, there are in the long run only analytic propositions. It would seem that for Leibniz truths of fact are ultimately reducible to truths of reason. That is to say, to analytic propositions, at least for an omniscient mind. Well, I couldn't agree with that. For one thing it would fail to meet the requirements of the experience of freedom. I don't want to uphold the whole philosophy of Leibniz. I have made use of his argument from contingent to necessary being, basing the argument on the principle of sufficient reason, simply because it seems to me a brief and clear formulation of what is, in my opinion, the fundamental metaphysical argument for God's existence.

**R:** But, to my mind, "a necessary proposition" has got to be analytic. I don't see what else it can mean. And analytic propositions are always complex and logically somewhat late. "Irrational animals are animals" is an analytic proposition; but a proposition such as "This is an animal" can never be analytic. In fact, all the propositions that can be analytic are somewhat late in the build-up of propositions.

**C:** Take the proposition "if there is a contingent being then there is a necessary being." I consider that that proposition hypothetically expressed is a necessary proposition. If you are going to call every necessary proposition an analytic proposition, then — in order to avoid a dispute in terminology — I would agree to call it analytic, though I don't consider it a tautological proposition. But the proposition is a necessary proposition only on the supposition that there is a contingent being. That there is a contingent being actually existing has to be discovered by experience, and the proposition that there is a contingent being is certainly not an analytic proposition, though once you know, I should maintain, that there is a contingent being, it follows of necessity that there is a necessary being.

**R:** The difficulty of this argument is that I don't admit the idea of a necessary being and I don't admit that there is any particular meaning in calling other beings "contingent." These phrases don't for me have a significance except within a logic that I reject.

**C:** Do you mean that you reject these terms because they won't fit in with what is called "modern logic"?

**R:** Well, I can't find anything that they could mean. The word "necessary," it seems to me, is a useless word, except as applied to analytic propositions, not to things.

**C:** In the first place, what do you mean by "modern logic"? As far as I know, there are somewhat differing systems. In the second place, not all modern logicians surely would admit the meaninglessness of metaphysics. We both know, at any rate, one very eminent modern thinker whose knowledge of modern logic was profound, but who certainly did not think that metaphysics are meaningless or, in particular, that the problem of God is meaningless. Again, even if all modern logicians held that metaphysical terms are meaningless, it would not follow that they were right. The proposition that metaphysical terms are meaningless seems to me to be a proposition based on an assumed philosophy.

The dogmatic position behind it seems to be this: What will not go into my machine is non-existent, or it is meaningless; it is the expression of emotion. I am simply trying to point out that anybody who says that a particular system of modern logic is the sole criterion of meaning is saying something that is over-dogmatic; he is dogmatically insisting that a part of philosophy is the whole of philosophy. After all, a "contingent" being is a being which has not in itself the complete reason for its existence – that's what I mean by a contingent being. You know, as well as I do, that the existence of neither of us can be explained without reference to something or somebody outside us, our parents, for example. A "necessary" being, on the other hand means a being that must and cannot not exist. You may say that there is no such being, but you will find it hard to convince me that you do not understand the terms I am using. If you do not understand them, then how can you be entitled to say that such a being does not exist, if that is what you do say?

**R:** Well, there are points here that I don't propose to go into at length. I don't maintain the meaninglessness of metaphysics in general at all. I maintain the meaninglessness of certain particular terms – not on any general ground, but simply because I've not been able to see an interpretation of those particular terms. It's not a general dogma – it's a particular thing. But those points I will leave out for the moment. And I will say that what you have been saying brings us back, it seems to me, to the ontological argument that there is a being whose essence involves existence, so that his existence is analytic. That seems to me to be impossible, and it raises, of course, the question what one means by existence, and as to this, I think a subject named can never be significantly said to exist but only a subject described. And that existence, in fact, quite definitely is not a predicate.

**C:** Well, you say, I believe, that it is bad grammar, or rather bad syntax to say for example "T. S. Eliot exists"; one ought to say, for example, "He, the author of *Murder in the Cathedral*, exists." Are you going to say that the proposition, "The cause of the world exists," is without meaning? You may say that the world has no cause; but I fail to see how you can say that the proposition that "the cause of the world exists" is meaningless. Put it in the form of a question: "Has the world a cause?" or "Does a cause of the world exist?" Most people surely would understand the question, even if they don't agree about the answer.

**R:** Well, certainly the question "Does the cause of the world exist?" is a question that has meaning. But if you say "Yes, God is the cause of the world" you're using God as a proper name; then "God exists" will not be a statement that has meaning; that is the position that I'm maintaining. Because, therefore, it will follow that it cannot be an analytic proposition ever to say that this or that exists. For example, suppose you take as your subject "the existent round-square," it would look like an analytic proposition that "the existent round-square exists," but it doesn't exist.

**C:** No, it doesn't, then surely you can't say it doesn't exist unless you have a conception of what existence is. As to the phrase "existent round-square," I should say that it has no meaning at all.

**R:** I quite agree. Then I should say the same thing in another context in reference to a "necessary being."

**C:** Well, we seem to have arrived at an impasse. To say that a necessary being is a being that must exist and cannot not exist has for me a definite meaning. For you it has no meaning.

**R:** Well, we can press the point a little, I think. A being that must exist and cannot not exist, would surely, according to you, be a being whose essence involves existence.

**C:** Yes, a being the essence of which is to exist. But I should not be willing to argue the existence of God simply from the idea of His essence because I don't think we have any clear intuition of God's essence as yet. I think we have to argue from the world of experience to God.

**R:** Yes, I quite see the distinction. But, at the same time, for a being with sufficient knowledge, it would be true to say "Here is this being whose essence involves existence!".

**C:** Yes, certainly if anybody saw God, he would see that God must exist.

**R:** So that I mean there is a being whose essence involves existence although we don't know that essence. We only know there is such a being.

**C:** Yes, I should add we don't know the essence *a priori*. It is only *a posteriori* through our experience of the world that we come to a knowledge of the existence of that being. And then one argues, the essence and existence must be identical. Because if God's essence and God's existence was not identical, then some sufficient reason for this existence would have to be found beyond God.

**R:** So it all turns on this question of sufficient reason, and I must say you haven't defined "sufficient reason" in a way that I can understand – what do you mean by sufficient reason? You don't mean cause?

**C:** Not necessarily. Cause is a kind of sufficient reason. Only contingent beings can have a cause. God is His own sufficient reason; and He is not cause of Himself. By sufficient reason in the full sense I mean an explanation adequate for the existence of some particular being.

**R:** But when is an explanation adequate? Suppose I am about to make a flame with a match. You may say that the adequate explanation of that is that I rub it on the box.

**C:** Well, for practical purposes – but theoretically, that is only a partial explanation. An adequate explanation must ultimately be a total explanation, to which nothing further can be added.

**R:** Then I can only say that you're looking for something which can't be got, and which one ought not to expect to get.

**C:** To say that one has not found it is one thing; to say that one should not look for it seems to me rather dogmatic.

**R:** Well, I don't know. I mean, the explanation of one thing is another thing which makes the other thing dependent on yet another, and you have to grasp this sorry scheme of things entire to do what you want, and that we can't do.

**C:** But are you going to say that we can't, or we shouldn't even raise the question of the existence of the whole of this sorry scheme of things – of the whole universe?

**R:** Yes, I don't think there's any meaning in it at all. I think the word "universe" is a handy word in some connections, but I don't think it stands for anything that has a meaning.

**C:** If the word is meaningless, it can't be so very handy. In any case, I don't say that the universe is something different from the objects which compose it (I indicated that in my brief summary of the proof), what I'm doing is to look for the reason, in this case the cause of the objects – the real or imagined totality of which constitute what we call the universe. You say, I think that the universe – or my existence if you prefer, or any other existence – is unintelligible?

**R:** First may I take up the point that if a word is meaningless it can't be handy. That sounds well but isn't in fact correct. Take, say, such a word as "the" or "than." You can't point to any object that those words mean, but they are very useful words; I should say the same of "universe." But leaving that point, you ask whether I consider that the universe is unintelligible. I shouldn't say unintelligible – I think it is without explanation. Intelligible, to my mind, is a different thing. Intelligible has to do with the thing itself intrinsically and not with its relations.

**C:** Well, my point is that what we call the world is intrinsically unintelligible, apart from the existence of God. You see, I don't believe that the infinity of the series of events – I mean a horizontal series, so to speak – if such an infinity could be proved, would be in the slightest degree relevant to the situation. If you add up chocolates you get chocolates after all and not a sheep. If you add up chocolates to infinity, you presumably get an infinite number of chocolates. So if you add up contingent beings to infinity, you still get contingent beings, not a necessary being. An infinite series of contingent beings will be, to my way of thinking, as unable to cause itself as one contingent being. However, you say, I think, that it is illegitimate to raise the question of what will explain the existence of any particular object?

**R:** It's quite all right if you mean by explaining it, simply finding a cause for it.

**C:** Well, why stop at one particular object? Why shouldn't one raise the question of the cause of the existence of all particular objects?

**R:** Because I see no reason to think there is any. The whole concept of cause is one we derive from our observation of particular things; I see no reason whatsoever to suppose that the total has any cause whatsoever.

**C:** Well, to say that there isn't any cause is not the same thing as saying that we shouldn't look for a cause. The statement that there isn't any cause should come, if it comes at all, at the end of the inquiry, not the beginning. In any case, if the total has no cause, then to my way of thinking it must be its own cause, which seems to me impossible. Moreover, the statement that the world is simply there if in answer to a question, presupposes that the question has meaning.

**R:** No, it doesn't need to be its own cause, what I'm saying is that the concept of cause is not applicable to the total.

**C:** Then you would agree with Sartre that the universe is what he calls "gratuitous"?

**R:** Well, the word "gratuitous" suggests that it might be something else; I should say that the universe is just there, and that's all.

**C:** Well, I can't see how you can rule out the legitimacy of asking the question how the total, or anything at all comes to be there. Why something rather than nothing, that is the question? The fact that we gain our knowledge of causality empirically, from particular causes, does not rule out the possibility of asking what the cause of the series is. If the word "cause" were meaningless or if it could be shown that Kant's view of the matter were correct, the question would be illegitimate I agree; but you don't seem to hold that the word "cause" is meaningless, and I do not suppose you are a Kantian.

**R:** I can illustrate what seems to me your fallacy. Every man who exists has a mother, and it seems to me your argument is that therefore the human race must have a mother, but obviously the human race hasn't a mother – that's a different logical sphere.

**C:** Well, I can't really see any parity. If I were saying "every object has a phenomenal cause, therefore, the whole series has a phenomenal cause," there would be a parity; but I'm not saying that; I'm saying, every object has a phenomenal cause if you insist on the infinity of the series – but the series of phenomenal causes is an insufficient explanation of the series. Therefore, the series has not a phenomenal cause but a transcendent cause.

**R:** That's always assuming that not only every particular thing in the world, but the world as a whole must have a cause. For that assumption I see no ground whatever. If you'll give me a ground I'll listen to it.

**C:** Well, the series of events is either caused or it's not caused. If it is caused, there must obviously be a cause outside the series. If it's not caused then it's sufficient to itself, and if it's sufficient to itself it is what I call necessary. But it can't be necessary since each member is contingent, and we've agreed that the total has no reality apart from its members, therefore, it can't be necessary. Therefore, it can't be – uncaused – therefore it must have a cause. And I should like to observe in passing that the statement "the world is simply there and is inexplicable" can't be got out of logical analysis.

**R:** I don't want to seem arrogant, but it does seem to me that I can conceive things that you say the human mind can't conceive. As for things not having a cause, the physicists assure us that individual quantum transitions in atoms have no cause.

**C:** Well, I wonder now whether that isn't simply a temporary inference.

**R:** It may be, but it does show that physicists' minds can conceive it.

**C:** Yes, I agree, some scientists – physicists – are willing to allow for indetermination within a restricted field. But very many scientists are not so willing. I think that Professor Dingle, of London University, maintains that the Heisenberg uncertainty principle tells us something about the success (or the lack of it) of the present atomic theory in correlating observations, but not about nature in itself, and many physicists would accept this view. In any case, I don't see how physicists can fail to accept the theory in practice, even if they don't do so in theory. I cannot see how science could be conducted on any other assumption than that of order and intelligibility in nature. The physicist presupposes, at least tacitly, that there is some sense in investigating nature and looking for the causes of events, just as the detective presupposes that there is some sense in looking for the cause of a murder. The metaphysician assumes that there is sense in looking for the reason or cause of phenomena, and, not being a Kantian, I consider that the metaphysician is as justified in his assumption as the physicist. When Sartre, for example, says that the world is gratuitous, I think that he has not sufficiently considered what is implied by "gratuitous."

**R:** I think – there seems to me a certain unwarrantable extension here; a physicist looks for causes; that does not necessarily imply that there are causes everywhere. A man may look for gold without assuming that there is gold everywhere; if he finds gold, well and good, if he doesn't he's had bad luck. The same is true when the physicists look for causes. As for Sartre, I don't profess to know what he means, and I shouldn't like to be thought to interpret him, but for my part, I do think the notion of the world having an explanation is a mistake. I don't see why one should expect it to have, and I think [what] you say about what the scientist assumes is an over-statement.

**C:** Well, it seems to me that the scientist does make some such assumption. When he experiments to find out some particular truth, behind that experiment lies the assumption that the universe is not simply discontinuous. There is the possibility of finding out a truth by experiment. The experiment may be a bad one, it may lead to no result, or not to the result that he wants, but that at any rate there is the possibility, through experiment, of finding out the truth that he assumes. And that seems to me to assume an ordered and intelligible universe.

**R:** I think you're generalizing more than is necessary. Undoubtedly the scientist assumes that this sort of thing is likely to be found and will often be found. He does not assume that it will be found, and that's a very important matter in modem physics.

**C:** Well, I think he does assume or is bound to assume it tacitly in practice. It may be that, to quote Professor Haldane, "when I light the gas under the kettle, some of the water molecules will fly off as vapour, and there is no way of finding out which will do so," but it doesn't follow necessarily that the idea of chance must be introduced except in relation to our knowledge.

**R:** No it doesn't – at least if I may believe what he says. He's finding out quite a lot of things – the scientist is finding out quite a lot of things that are happening in the world, which are, at first, beginnings of causal chains – first causes which haven't in themselves got causes. He does not assume that everything has a cause.

**C:** Surely that's a first cause within a certain selected field. It's a relatively first cause.

**R:** I don't think he'd say so. If there's a world in which most events, but not all, have causes, he will then be able to depict the probabilities and uncertainties by assuming that this particular event you're interested in probably has a cause. And since in any case you won't get more than probability that's good enough.

**C:** It may be that the scientist doesn't hope to obtain more than probability, but in raising the question he assumes that the question of explanation has a meaning. But your general point then, Lord Russell, is that it's illegitimate even to ask the question of the cause of the world?

**R:** Yes, that's my position.

**C:** If it's a question that for you has no meaning, it's of course very difficult to discuss it, isn't it?

**R:** Yes, it is very difficult. What do you say – shall we pass on to some other issue?

**Questions**

1. Explain the disagreement between Russell and Copleston about the idea of a 'necessary being'. What is Russell's view? What is Copleston's view?

2. Explain their disagreement about the idea of a 'cause of the world'.

3. Why do they decide to pass on to some other issue at the end of the passage?

4. Which of the two speakers' views is closer to your own opinion?

# Cosmological arguments: key points revision sheet

- According to the cosmological argument, the universe cannot account for its own existence. It cannot have started by itself. There must be a sufficient reason to explain it. It is contingent and therefore must depend on something which is necessary and does not need a cause.
- Aquinas has cosmological arguments as the first three of his Five Ways:

  1. The Unmoved Mover explains motion.
  2. The Uncaused Causer explains chains of cause and effect.
  3. Contingent things cannot come into existence by themselves, so they must have been started by something with necessary existence.

- The Kalam argument in Islam says that infinity cannot exist in actuality, so that the universe must have had a beginning and must have been started by something.
- Leibniz said everything must have a sufficient reason to explain its existence.
- Hume and Russell argued that not everything has to have a reason. Just because individual things within the universe have reasons for their existence, it does not mean that there must be a reason for the universe as a whole. It could be just a 'brute fact'.
- Russell and Copleston debated cosmological arguments on the radio. Copleston supported Aquinas' views, but Russell said that the whole idea of the universe having a reason was meaningless.
- Peter Atkins said that one day scientists will explain why the universe came into existence, and then there will be no need to explain it with reference to God.

# Cosmological arguments: revision test questions

1. Who took part in a radio debate against Bertrand Russell about the cosmological argument?

2. What is the name of the Islamic version of the cosmological argument?

3. Who used the example of an infinite library of books, to illustrate his ideas in support of the Islamic cosmological argument?

4. When Aquinas spoke about God as the 'efficient cause' of the universe, he was borrowing ideas from which ancient Greek philosopher?

5. What did Russell mean when he said that the universe was a 'brute fact'?

6. How did Hume criticise cosmological arguments?

7. Leibniz believed that there is a Principle of —— Reason. What is the missing word?

8. Who said that we should 'deny knowledge in order to make room for faith', and rejected the cosmological argument on the grounds that God is not available to human reason?

9. How many of Aquinas' Five Ways are versions of the cosmological argument?

# Cosmological arguments: revision test answers

1. F. R. Copleston

2. Kalam

3. William Lane Craig

4. Aristotle

5. He meant that it 'just is', without any need for an explanation.

6. He said that the existence of the universe could have had other causes; there is no reason to assume that the First Cause must be the God of Christianity; there is no need for the universe as a whole to have an explanation.

7. Sufficient

8. Kant

9. Three

# Cosmological arguments: practice exam question

Students' work should be measured against the Edexcel levels of response for AS Religious Studies.

**(a) Explain Aquinas' cosmological argument for the existence of God.**

AO1

For high marks in AO1, students should aim for relevance, clarity, accuracy and detail. Here, they should be able to explain how Aquinas approaches cosmological arguments in his Five Ways, using the three related arguments to reach the conclusion that there must be a First Cause which we call God. Good answers might mention the dependence of Aquinas on Aristotle, his rejection of the notion of infinite regress and his assumption that the universe and the things within it have a purpose.

**(b) How far does Aquinas' cosmological argument succeed in proving the existence of God?**

AO2

To achieve a high level, students should make an attempt at critical analysis. They should make reference to alternative different points of view and use balanced reasoning. Their arguments should be expressed accurately and fluently, and they should use a range of technical vocabulary. They should reach a conclusion which is well supported by the rest of the answer, rather than just tacked on at the end. Here, students might draw attention to the impossibility of reaching a firm proof through inductive reasoning. They might give criticisms of the argument based on the views of thinkers such as Hume and Russell. Better answers will assess the strength of these criticisms and reach a conclusion, rather than simply presenting criticisms without comment.

# Design and cosmological arguments: key vocabulary revision sheet

**Analogy** – is when similar things are compared as a way of clarifying or supporting a point.

**Anthropic principle** – the argument that the natural laws of the universe have been 'fine tuned' to allow human life to exist.

**Brute fact** – a fact that 'just is', without any explanation.

**Contingent** – depending on something else.

**Creationism** – the belief that the world and everything in it was made exactly as described in the Bible.

**Deductive arguments** – arguments that depend only on logic and not on experience. If the premises are true, then the conclusion is proved.

**Epistemic distance** – a distance in knowledge or awareness.

**Inductive arguments** – arguments that cannot prove, but they try to persuade by providing evidence from human experience in support of the conclusion.

**Infinite regress** – a chain going infinitely back without any beginning.

**Natural selection** – the process by which evolution is said to take place, through the survival of the fittest who pass on their genes to the next generation.

**Necessary (as in 'necessary existence')** – in this context, the word 'necessary' is used to mean the opposite of contingent. A necessary being has no cause and depends on nothing else for its continued existence.

**Sceptic** – someone who is inclined to doubt what he or she is told or wishes to suspend judgement unless there is certainty; someone who is keen to point out the limitations of knowledge.

**Teleological** – looking at the 'tail end', or end result, in order to draw conclusions.

# Discussion: natural and moral evil

Traditionally, philosophers have claimed that 'natural' evil is that which is not humanity's fault: suffering is caused because of the way things are in the natural world. 'Moral' evil is that which results from humanity's propensity to sin: where suffering is caused by human wickedness.

**Decide whether the following are examples of natural evil, moral evil, neither, or a mixture of both:**

- the earthquake in South Asia in 2005
- a murder committed by someone with a mental illness
- lung cancer in a non-smoker
- pain in childbirth
- flooding in Bangladesh
- football hooliganism
- the Great Fire of London
- the attack on the Twin Towers in New York on 11 September 2001
- famine in developing countries
- the AIDS epidemic in Africa
- global warming
- a child with measles

**Can you think of an example of evil that is purely natural, and an example that is purely moral?**

# Problem of evil: evaluating some solutions

Consider these different explanations of why moral evil occurs.

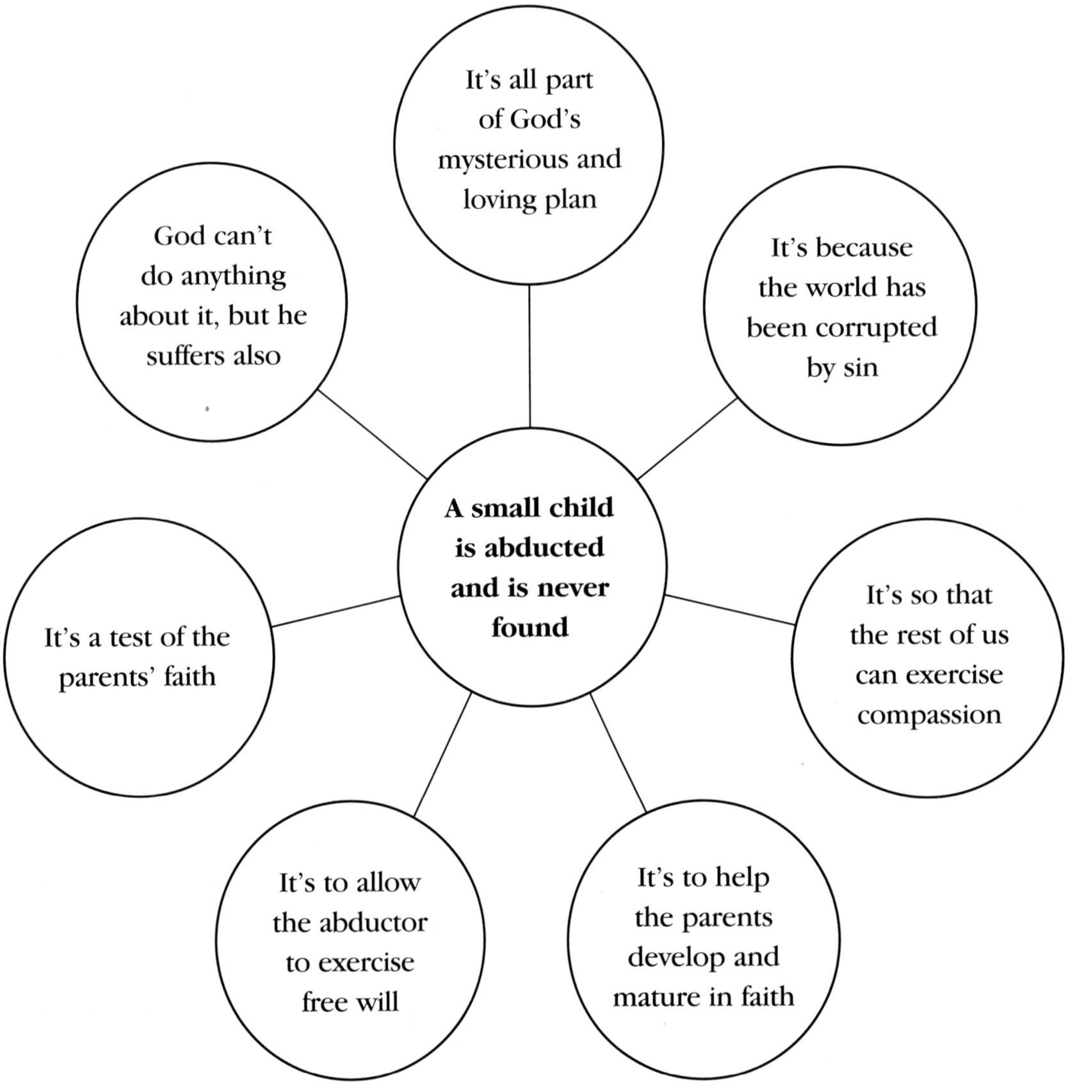


- How successful are they in addressing the problem of evil?
- Which are the most/least acceptable responses?
- What questions do they raise?
- Are there any other responses which might be more acceptable?

# Excerpt from *The Brothers Karamazov*

**Fyoder Dostoevsky's 1880 novel, *The Brothers Karamazov* is a story of family tensions and rivalries. In this famous scene from chapter 35, Ivan Karamazov visits his younger brother Alyosha, who is a novice monk. Ivan challenges his brother's faith by giving him examples of innocent suffering – the suffering of children and of animals. He puts to his brother the view that even if all this suffering happens in order to bring about eternal harmony, eternal harmony simply isn't worth the price.**

I simply wanted to show you my point of view. I meant to speak of the suffering of mankind generally, but we had better confine ourselves to the sufferings of the children. That reduces the scope of my argument to a tenth of what it would be. Still we'd better keep to the children, though it does weaken my case. But, in the first place, children can be loved even at close quarters, even when they are dirty, even when they are ugly (I fancy, though, children never are ugly). The second reason why I won't speak of grown-up people is that, besides being disgusting and unworthy of love, they have a compensation – they've eaten the apple and know good and evil, and they have become 'like gods'. They go on eating it still. But the children haven't eaten anything, and are so far innocent. Are you fond of children, Alyosha? I know you are, and you will understand why I prefer to speak of them. If they, too, suffer horribly on earth, they must suffer for their fathers' sins, they must be punished for their fathers, who have eaten the apple; but that reasoning is of the other world and is incomprehensible for the heart of man here on earth. The innocent must not suffer for another's sins, and especially such innocents!

Our historical pastime is the direct satisfaction of inflicting pain. There are lines in Nekrassov describing how a peasant lashes a horse on the eyes, 'on its meek eyes', everyone must have seen it. It's peculiarly Russian. He describes how a feeble little nag has foundered under too heavy a load and cannot move. The peasant beats it, beats it savagely, beats it at last not knowing what he is doing in the intoxication of cruelty, thrashes it mercilessly over and over again. 'However weak you are, you must pull, if you die for it'. The nag strains, and then he begins lashing the poor defenceless creature on its weeping, on its 'meek eyes'. The frantic beast tugs and draws the load, trembling all over, gasping for breath, moving sideways, with a sort of unnatural spasmodic action – it's awful in Nekrassov. But that's only a horse, and God has horses to be beaten.

This poor child of five was subjected to every possible torture by those cultivated parents. They beat her, thrashed her, kicked her for no reason till her body was one bruise. Then, they went to greater refinements of cruelty – shut her up all night in the cold and frost in a privy, and because she didn't ask to be taken up at night (as though a child of five sleeping its angelic, sound sleep could be trained to wake and ask), they smeared her face and filled her mouth with excrement, and it was her mother, her mother did this. And that mother could sleep, hearing the poor child's groans! Can you understand why a little creature, who can't even understand what's done to her, should beat her little aching heart with her tiny fist in the dark and the cold, and weep her meek unresentful tears to dear, kind God to protect her? Do you understand that, friend and brother, you pious and humble novice? Do you understand why this infamy must be and is permitted? Without it, I am told, man could not have existed on earth, for he could not have known good and evil. Why should he know that diabolical good and evil when it costs so much? Why, the whole world of knowledge is not worth that child's prayer to 'dear, kind God'! I say nothing of the sufferings of grown-up people, they have eaten the apple, damn them, and the devil take them all! But these little ones! I am making you suffer, Alyosha, you are not yourself. I'll leave off if you like.

'Never mind. I want to suffer too', muttered Alyosha.

One picture, only one more, because it's so curious, so characteristic, and I have only just read it in some collection of Russian antiquities. I've forgotten the name. I must look it up. It was in the darkest days of serfdom at the beginning of the century, and long live the Liberator of the People! There was in those days a general of aristocratic connections, the owner of great estates, one of those men – somewhat exceptional, I believe, even then – who, retiring from the service into a life of leisure, are convinced that they've earned absolute power over the lives of their subjects. There were such men then. So our general, settled on his property of two thousand souls, lives in pomp, and domineers over his poor neighbours as though they were dependents and buffoons. He has kennels of hundreds of hounds and nearly a hundred dog-boys – all mounted, and in uniform. One day a serf-boy, a little child of eight, threw a stone in play and hurt the paw of the general's favourite hound. 'Why is my favourite dog lame?' He is told that the boy threw a stone that hurt the dog's paw. 'So you did it.' The general looked the child up and down. 'Take him.' He was taken – taken from his mother and kept shut up all night. Early that morning the general comes out on horseback, with the hounds, his dependents, dog-boys, and huntsmen, all mounted around him in full hunting parade. The servants are summoned for their edification, and in front of them all stands the mother of the child. The child is brought from the lock-up. It's a gloomy, cold, foggy, autumn day, a capital day for hunting. The general orders the child to be undressed; the child is stripped naked. He shivers, numb with terror, not daring to cry... 'Make him run,' commands the general. 'Run! run!' shout the dog-boys. The boy runs... 'At him!' yells the general, and he sets the whole pack of hounds on the child. The hounds catch him, and tear him to pieces before his mother's eyes! ... I believe the general was afterwards declared incapable of administering his estates. Well – what did he deserve? To be shot? To be shot for the satisfaction of our moral feelings? Speak, Alyosha!'

'To be shot,' murmured Alyosha, lifting his eyes to Ivan with a pale, twisted smile.

'Bravo!' cried Ivan delighted. 'If even you say so... – You're a pretty monk! So there is a little devil sitting in your heart, Alyosha Karamazov!'

'What I said was absurd, but...'

'That's just the point, that "but"!' cried Ivan. 'Let me tell you, novice, that the absurd is only too necessary on earth. The world stands on absurdities, and perhaps nothing would have come to pass in it without them. We know what we know!'

'What do you know?'

'I understand nothing,' Ivan went on, as though in delirium. 'I don't want to understand anything now. I want to stick to the fact. I made up my mind long ago not to understand. If I try to understand anything, I shall be false to the fact, and I have determined to stick to the fact.'

If all must suffer to pay for the eternal harmony, what have children to do with it, tell me, please? It's beyond all comprehension why they should suffer, and why they should pay for the harmony. Why should they, too, furnish material to enrich the soil for the harmony of the future?

I don't want harmony. From love for humanity I don't want it. I would rather be left with the unavenged suffering. I would rather remain with my unavenged suffering and unsatisfied indignation, even if I were wrong. Besides, too high a price is asked for harmony; it's beyond our means to pay so much to enter on it. And so I hasten to give back my entrance ticket, and if I am an honest man I am bound to give it back as soon as possible. And that I am doing. It's not God that I don't accept, Alyosha, only I most respectfully return him the ticket.

'That's rebellion,' murmured Alyosha, looking down.

'Rebellion? I am sorry you call it that,' said Ivan earnestly. 'One can hardly live in rebellion, and I want to live. Tell me yourself, I challenge your answer. Imagine that you are creating a fabric of human destiny with the object of making men happy in the end, giving them peace and rest at last, but that it was essential and inevitable to torture to death only one tiny creature – that baby beating its breast with its fist, for instance – and to found that edifice on its unavenged tears, would you consent to be the architect on those conditions? Tell me, and tell the truth.'

'No, I wouldn't consent,' said Alyosha softly.

**Questions**

1. Why does Ivan use examples of animal suffering and of children suffering, rather than adults?

2. Ivan's conclusion is that if the world has to contain suffering, God should not have made it at all. Would you agree with him? Why, or why not?

# Problem of evil: should God have made a world in which suffering was more limited?

Clearly if there is a God, he must set a limit to the amount of suffering. Clearly too there is such a limit. There is a temporal limit constituted by death to the amount a given man can suffer. And there is also presumably a limit to the intensity of possible suffering, set by the constitution of the brain through which suffering comes to man. But the objection is that the limit is set too wide. It ought never to have allowed Hiroshima, Belsen, the Lisbon Earthquake, or the Black Death. But the trouble is that the fewer natural evils God provides, the less opportunity he provides for man to exercise responsibility. For the less natural evil, the less knowledge he gives to man of how to produce or avoid suffering and disaster, the less opportunity for his exercise of the higher virtues, and the less experience of the harsh possibilities of existence; and the less he allows men the opportunity to bring about large-scale horrors, the less the freedom and responsibility which he gives to them. What in effect the objection is asking is that God should make a toy-world, a world where things matter, but not very much; where we can choose and our choices can make a small difference, but the real choices remain God's. For he simply would not allow us the choice of doing real harm, or through our negligence allow real harm to occur. He would be like the over-protective parent who will not let his child out of his sight for a moment.

(from Richard Swinburne, *The Existence of God*, Clarendon Press, 2004)

**Questions**

1. How does Swinburne answer the objection that God should have set a limit on human suffering?

2. What reasons does Swinburne give for God having allowed Hiroshima, Belsen and other cases of mass suffering?

3. What criticisms might be made of Swinburne's argument?

4. To what extent is Swinburne's argument persuasive, in your view?

# Problem of evil: key points revision sheet

- The problem of evil is the problem of reconciling the existence of evil and suffering with the existence of an omnipotent, loving God.
- Moral evil is the evil people cause by their own deliberate choices. Natural evil is not caused by human fault but by the way the earth is made.
- Theodicies are attempts to justify God in spite of the existence of evil.
- The book of Job suggests that evil is sent by God as a test of faith.
- Some people think the Devil is responsible for evil, but this does not solve the problem of why God made the Devil and why God allows the Devil to do anything.
- Muslims believe that suffering is a test and that everything is controlled by Allah.
- Hindus and Buddhists believe that suffering is the result of karma. There is no such thing as innocent suffering, it all results from behaviour in past lives.
- Augustine taught that evil and suffering came into the world as a result of the fall of thc angels – but why did God allow the angels to do wrong in the first place?
- Irenaeus taught that evil is part of the world for our own good so that we can grow and mature spiritually. His view is supported by Hick and Swinburne. But why do some people suffer so much more than others, and why did God not make us mature to start with?
- The 'free will defence' says that we have to have a real choice between good and evil if we are to make truly free decisions.
- Process theologians give up the idea that God is completely omnipotent, and suggest that God suffers along with us and cannot change the natural laws of the world or force our moral choices.

# Problem of evil: revision test questions

1. In the book of Job, why does Job suffer?

2. When Job meets with God in order to ask about his suffering, what answer does he get?

3. What is the different between natural and moral evil?

4. In the story of the Fall of Adam and Eve, what was it that Adam and Eve were forbidden to do?

5. In Dostoevsky's *The Brothers Karamazov*, why does Ivan return his 'entrance ticket'?

6. Which Christian thinker suggested that some of the angels fell because they received less grace than others?

7. What does it mean to call evil a '*privatio boni*'?

8. Who called the world a 'vale of soul-making', using words from Keats?

9. Give an argument against the Augustinian theodicy.

10. Give an argument against the Irenaean theodicy.

11. What does process theology suggest as a response to the problem of evil?

12. Give an example of a thinker who argued that this is the best of all possible worlds.

# Problem of evil: revision test answers

1. Because Satan wants to test Job's faithfulness, and God agrees.

2. Job cannot do the things God can do, and cannot expect to know the reasons why he suffers.

3. Natural evil is caused by the way the natural world is and is not humanity's fault, but moral evil is caused by human sin.

4. Eat from the tree in the middle of the garden/the tree of the knowledge of good and evil.

5. Because he does not want to be part of a world where evil is necessary.

6. Augustine

7. Evil is a lack of goodness, it does not have any real existence of its own.

8. John Hick

9. Accept any reasonable answer, e.g. that modern people do not believe in angels; that we still need an explanation of how perfect beings came to fall; that God could have stopped it.

10. Accept any reasonable answer, e.g. that free will is not worth the suffering, that some people suffer a lot more than others, that some suffer without being able to learn, that God could have made us perfect to start with.

11. It gives up the idea of God as omnipotent and argues that God suffers alongside us and does not know the future.

12. Accept any reasonable response, such as Leibniz, Swinburne, Hick.

# Discussion: what is a miracle?

**Which of the following would you consider to be a miracle (if any)? Why, or why not?**

1. Sarah was very close to her grandmother, but sadly her grandmother died. Later, Sarah dreamed that her grandmother spoke to her and told her that she shouldn't be unhappy any more; after this dream, Sarah began to get over her grief.

2. Rob was painting his bedroom window frame, when the pot of paint fell off the ladder and spilt all over his expensive new carpet. The paint splash looked just like a silhouette of Jesus on the cross.

3. Louise was dangerously ill with a brain tumour, and doctors said that she had only a ten per cent chance of recovery. Her friends at church raised the money to take her to Lourdes. When she came back from her pilgrimage, she began to respond well to treatment, and despite the gloomy predictions, eventually she made a full recovery.

4. Rebecca was also dangerously ill with a brain tumour just like Louise's. Her friends at church also raised money, and she too went to Lourdes. The day after she came back from her pilgrimage, doctors were astonished to find that she was in perfect health with no trace of having ever had a brain tumour. They had never seen anything like it before, and were unable to explain it.

5. Amir decided to make a parachute jump for charity. Unfortunately, the parachute failed to open. Fortunately, Amir landed on the only pile of soft hay for miles around, and equally fortunately, there was no pitchfork in it, so he was completely unharmed.

6. Mary and Tom desperately wanted children, but after eight years, they had no success in conceiving. After praying about it, they had IVF treatment, and although they had been warned that success was not guaranteed, Mary became pregnant and gave birth to healthy twins, a boy and a girl.

# Biblical miracles: worksheet

**Familiarise yourself with some biblical miracle stories to use as examples in your written work. Look up the passages and make notes about them**

**From the Old Testament**

**Exodus 3:1–6**

- What happens in the story?
- What, in the story, happens which goes beyond the laws of nature? (v.2)
- What was the point of God performing this miracle, according to the biblical writer?

**Exodus 9:22–25**

- What happens in the story?
- Why is this event interpreted as a miracle?

**Exodus 14:21–25**

- What happens in the story?
- What does the story try to show about the nature of God?

**2 Kings 2: 11–12**

- What happens in the story?
- What is this story meant to show about the nature of God and the status of Elijah?

**2 Kings 5:1–14**

- What happens in the story?
- Why is this event interpreted as a sign from God rather than just someone getting better?

**Daniel 6:16–23**

- What happens in the story?
- Why does this miracle happen, according to the writer?

**Jonah 1:17–2:1 and 2:10**

• What happens in these verses, and how are the laws of nature transcended?

**From the New Testament**

**Matthew 1:18**

• What happens here, and what is being implied about the child who is to come?

**Matthew 8:14–17**

• What kinds of miracles happen here, and what is the point of them said to be?

**Mark 2:3–12**

• What sort of miracle is this, and what reason does Mark give for its performance?

**Mark 6: 45–52**

• What is this miracle story about?

• What was the point of this happening, according to the writer?

**Luke 8:40–2, 49–56**

• What happens in the story? Why were the parents so amazed?

**Luke 9:12– 17**

• What happens in the story, and why does Luke include it in the Gospel?

**John 2:1–11**

• What happens in the story, and what reason does John give in v.11 for the event and others like it?

**John 20:11–18**

• What happens in the story?

For all the New Testament stories: Why is it important to the gospel writers to portray Jesus as a miracle worker?

# Miracles: key points revision sheet

- Some central religious teachings depend on belief in miracle, e.g. the Passover, the resurrection of Jesus.

- Different people define miracles in different ways. Some, e.g. Hume, say that miracles break the laws of nature. Others, e.g. John Macquarrie, say that they do not have to break the laws of nature but God has to be in the event in a special way, influencing the outcome.

- Calling something a 'miracle' involves putting a religious interpretation on events.

- Aquinas divided miracles into different kinds:

  1. Things that God does but nature can never do.
  2. Occasions where God changes the natural order of events.
  3. Occasions where God does something nature can do, but by-passes the laws of nature.

- Hume criticised belief in miracles because:

  - Sensible people always go for the natural, rather than the supernatural, explanation.
  - Miracles are only called miracles because they break the laws of nature. But the laws of nature are laws which always operate, so miracles never happen.
  - Reports of miracles come from ignorant and barbarous nations.
  - Miracle stories from different religions contradict each other.

- Bultmann suggested taking the miracle stories out of the Bible to make it more accessible for modern people to believe.

- Maurice Wiles argued that God does not do miracles for some people while ignoring others – this would be a cruel and arbitrary God. God acts in the world in a different way, through human behaviour.

# Miracles: revision test questions

1. Give examples of two miracle stories from the Gospels.

2. Give examples of two miracle stories from the Old Testament.

3. What did Aquinas think was the highest-ranking kind of miracle?

4. Why did some people argue that the first miracle officially attributed to Mother Teresa was not a miracle at all?

5. How does Hume define a miracle?

6. Why did Hume think that no reasonable person would believe that a miracle had happened?

7. Name a modern scholar who would agree with Hume in his rejection of miracle.

8. Who thought that the miracle stories were a barrier to faith and that the Bible should be 'demythologised' to take them out?

9. What was the name of the book by Maurice Wiles which rejected the idea that God performs occasional miracles?

10. Why did Wiles reject belief in occasional miracles?

# Miracles: revision test answers

1 and 2. There are many possiblities, such as healing stories (e.g.paralytic man in the Gospels, the healing of Naaman), miracles showing power over nature (e.g. calming of the storm, parting of the Red Sea) or miracles bringing the dead back to life (e.g. Lazarus, Jairus' daughter); accept any reasonable answer.

3. Things that God does but nature can never do.

4. Because the woman was receiving medical treatment as well and there was a natural explanation; because the evidence was not sound.

5. 'A miracle may be accurately defined, a transgression of a law of nature by a particular volition of the Deity or by the interposition of some invisible agent.'

6. Because the natural explanation will always be more likely; because laws of nature are laws and so they are not broken.

7. Many to choose from: Mackie, Dawkins, Flew, Russell, and so on.

8. Bultmann

9. *God's Action in the World*

10. Because they suggest an arbitrary God who could help people but chooses not to.

# Revision game: key vocabulary for Unit 1

For this game, you need to copy the following pages onto thin card and cut out the boxes to make individual cards.

You also need some means of timing accurately to the second – a stopwatch or wall clock with a second hand or an egg-timer perhaps.

**To play**

Divide the class into teams and give out the cards equally among them. Do not allow the team members to look at them yet. Ask each team to elect a spokesperson to take the cards from the pack and once the clock is started, to describe one by one the word or words on the card. The rest of the team must guess what the word is, by calling out suggestions. When the team has guessed correctly, the spokesperson can move on to the next card. When all the words have been correctly guessed, stop the clock. The winning team is the one to name all their cards in the fastest time.

- The spokesperson may not use the word on the card in any form (e.g. if the word was 'fisherman', the spokesperson could not say 'catches fish' or 'fishing').
- The word may not be spelled out.
- The spokesperson may say 'one word' or 'two words' etc, or 'one syllable' etc.
- The spokesperson may mime actions, but not mouth the words on the cards.
- If the team cannot guess the word and give up, a time penalty is added on to their score.

| | |
|---|---|
| **analogy** | **Dawkins** |
| **contingent** | **Hume** |
| **Paley** | **epistemic distance** |
| **infinite regress** | **Copleston** |
| **Five Ways** | **Russell** |
| **Darwin** | **Irenaeus** |
| **Aquinas** | **Augustine** |
| **Mill** | **Tennant** |

| | |
|---|---|
| **teleological** | **kalam** |
| **sceptic** | **Leibniz** |
| **natural selection** | **theodicy** |
| ***The Blind Watchmaker*** | **karma** |
| ***Summa Theologica*** | **moral evil** |
| **anthropic principle** | **Job** |
| **natural theology** | **process theology** |
| **Swinburne** | **Hick** |

# Religious experience: *The Miracle of Theism*

Whether (the content of religious experience) has any objective truth is the crucial further question. Certainly no demonstrative argument will establish this. The issue is whether the hypothesis that there objectively is something more gives a better explanation of the whole range of phenomena than can be given without it. James himself thinks that it does; yet he gives no real argument to support this opinion. This is, obviously, a less economical hypothesis than its naturalistic rival … all that has been shown goes against even this modest and indeterminate supernaturalism. The undeniable real causal source of these impulses may be normally 'unseen' and not understood or articulately reported; but it is eminently understandable and it belongs well within the same 'dimensions of existence' as other, wholly familiar, mental phenomena.
(from J. L. Mackie, *The Miracle of Theism*, Oxford University Press, 1982)

**Questions**

1. How might we judge which explanation of a religious experience is a 'better' one?

2. What does he mean by an 'economical' hypothesis? Why might he judge a theistic interpretation of religious experience to be less economical than a naturalistic interpretation?

3. Mackie assumes that the 'real' cause of religious experience is both 'undeniable' and 'eminently understandable'. To what extent would you agree with his view?

4. How might a theist, such as Richard Swinburne, respond to Mackie?

# Revelation through dreams

Look up and familiarise yourself with these examples of biblical dreams:

- Genesis 28:11–19
- Genesis 46:1–4
- Genesis 41: 1–7, 25–30
- Genesis 46:1–4
- Daniel 2:1–3, 2:25–28
- Matthew 1:20–21
- Matthew 2: 9–12
- Matthew 2:13
- Matthew 2:19–20
- Matthew 2:22

1. What is the purpose of the dream in each narrative (for example, does it act as a warning, or as a means of clarifying puzzling events, or something else)?

2. Some of the dreams use symbols which then have to be interpreted – find some examples of these.

3. How might a person know that a dream was from God, rather than just an ordinary dream?

4. How might a non-religious person account for dreams where the dreamers firmly believe that they have received revelation from God?

Suggested further reading: Sigmund Freud's *The Interpretation of Dreams* is worth dipping into. Freud suggested that dreams are a way in which the subconscious deals with issues that the conscious self suppresses while awake.

# Religious experience: Swinburne's Principle of Credulity

The Principle of Credulity is concerned with a subject's grounds for believing that things are as they seem to him. Clearly in ordinary life we use a wider principle, for we usually believe to have occurred what other people tell us that they perceived occurring. Other things being equal, we think that what others tell us they perceived, probably happened.

By 'other things being equal' I mean the absence of positive grounds for supposing that the others have misreported or misremembered their experiences, or that thing were not in fact as they seemed to those others to be. Clearly most of our beliefs about the world are based on what others claim to have perceived – beliefs about geography and history and science and everything else beyond immediate experience are thus based. We do not normally check that an informant is a reliable witness before accepting his reports. And we *could* not do so because we form our beliefs about they are saying, the meaning of the claims which they are making, on the assumption that other people normally tell the truth …

… One who has had a religious experience apparently of God has, by the Principle of Credulity, good reason for believing that there is a God – other things being equal – especially if it is a forceful experience.

(from Richard Swinburne, *The Existence of God*, Clarendon Press, 2004)

**Questions**

1. Is Swinburne right when he says that when other people tell us they perceived something to have happened, we usually assume that it really happened?

2. Is it reasonable to assume that other people normally tell us the truth?

3. If someone told you that he or she had seen a ghost, or a UFO, or had an 'out of body' experience, would you believe that he or she really had? Why, or why not?

4. Do you think Swinburne is right to argue that religious experience should be treated in the same way as sensory experience?

# Religious experience: *Revelations of Divine Love*

**Julian of Norwich (c.1342 – c.1416) lived as an anchoress in a cell next to the Church of St. Julian and St Edward in Norwich. When she was 30, she suffered a severe illness, and afterwards had intense religious experiences which she recorded in one of the first works ever to be written by a woman in English.**

In this same time our Lord shewed me a spiritual sight of His homely loving.

I saw that He is to us everything that is good and comfortable for us: He is our clothing that for love wrappeth us, claspeth us, and all encloseth us for tender love, that He may never leave us; being to us all-thing that is good, as to mine understanding.

Also in this He shewed me a little thing, the quantity of an hazel-nut, in the palm of my hand; and it was as round as a ball. I looked thereupon with eye of my understanding, and thought: What may this be? And it was answered generally thus: It is all that is made. I marvelled how it might last, for methought it might suddenly have fallen to naught for little[ness]. And I was answered in my understanding: It lasteth, and ever shall [last] for that God loveth it. And so All-thing hath the Being by the love of God.

In this Little Thing I saw three properties. The first is that God made it, the second is that God loveth it, the third, that God keepeth it. But what is to me verily the Maker, the Keeper, and the Lover, I cannot tell; for till I am Substantially oned to Him, I may never have full rest nor very bliss: that is to say, till I be so fastened to Him, that there is right nought that is made betwixt my God and me.

It needeth us to have knowing of the littleness of creatures and to hold as nought all-thing that is made, for to love and have God that is unmade. For this is the cause why we be not all in ease of heart and soul: that we seek here rest in those things that are so little, wherein is no rest, and know not our God that is All-mighty, All-wise, All-good. For He is the Very Rest. God willeth to be known, and it pleaseth Him that we rest in Him; for all that is beneath Him sufficeth not us. And this is the cause why that no soul is rested till it is made nought as to all things that are made. When it is willingly made nought, for love, to have Him that is all, then is it able to receive spiritual rest.

(from Julian of Norwich, *Revelations of Divine Love*, chapter 5)

# The Piper at the Gates of Dawn: a numinous experience

**In this extract from chapter 7 of *The Wind in the Willows*, Rat and Mole go out early to look for little Portly, a baby otter who has gone missing.**

Fastening their boat to a willow, the friends landed in this silent, silver kingdom, and patiently explored the hedges, the hollow trees, the runnels and their little culverts, the ditches and dry waterways. Embarking again and crossing over, they worked their way up the stream in this manner, while the moon, serene and detached in a cloudless sky, did what she could, though so far off, to help them in their quest; till her hour came and she sank earthwards reluctantly, and left them, and mystery once more held field and river.

Then a change began slowly to declare itself. The horizon became clearer, field and tree came more into sight, and somehow with a different look; the mystery began to drop away from them. A bird piped suddenly, and was still; and a light breeze sprang up and set the reeds and bulrushes rustling. Rat, who was in the stern of the boat, while Mole sculled, sat up suddenly and listened with a passionate intentness. Mole, who with gentle strokes was just keeping the boat moving while he scanned the banks with care, looked at him with curiosity.

'It's gone!' sighed the Rat, sinking back in his seat again. 'So beautiful and strange and new. Since it was to end so soon, I almost wish I had never heard it. For it has roused a longing in me that is pain, and nothing seems worth while but just to hear that sound once more and go on listening to it for ever. No! There it is again!' he cried, alert once more. Entranced, he was silent for a long space, spellbound.

'Now it passes on and I begin to lose it,' he said presently. 'O Mole! the beauty of it! The merry bubble and joy, the thin, clear, happy call of the distant piping! Such music I never dreamed of, and the call in it is stronger even than the music is sweet! Row on, Mole, row! For the music and the call must be for us.'

The Mole, greatly wondering, obeyed. 'I hear nothing myself,' he said, 'but the wind playing in the reeds and rushes and osiers.'

The Rat never answered, if indeed he heard. Rapt, transported, trembling, he was possessed in all his senses by this new divine thing that caught up his helpless soul and swung and dandled it, a powerless but happy infant in a strong sustaining grasp.

In silence Mole rowed steadily, and soon they came to a point where the river divided, a long backwater branching off to one side. With a slight movement of his head Rat, who had long dropped the rudder-lines, directed the rower to take the backwater. The creeping tide of light gained and gained, and now they could see the colour of the flowers that gemmed the water's edge.

'Clearer and nearer still,' cried the Rat joyously. 'Now you must surely hear it! Ah – at last – I see you do!'

Breathless and transfixed the Mole stopped rowing as the liquid run of that glad piping broke on him like a wave, caught him up, and possessed him utterly. He saw the tears on his comrade's cheeks, and bowed his head and understood. For a space they hung there, brushed by the purple loose-strife that fringed the bank; then the clear imperious summons that marched hand-in-hand with the intoxicating melody imposed its will on Mole, and mechanically he bent to his oars again. And the light grew steadily stronger, but no birds sang as they were wont to do at the approach of dawn; and but for the heavenly music all was marvellously still.

On either side of them, as they glided onwards, the rich meadow-grass seemed that morning of a freshness and a greenness unsurpassable. Never had they noticed the roses so vivid, the willow-herb so riotous, the meadow-sweet so odorous and pervading. Then the murmur of the approaching weir began to hold the air, and they felt a consciousness that they were nearing the end, whatever it might be, that surely awaited their expedition.

A wide half-circle of foam and glinting lights and shining shoulders of green water, the great weir closed the backwater from bank to bank, troubled all the quiet surface with twirling eddies and floating foam-streaks, and deadened all other sounds with its solemn and soothing rumble. In midmost of the stream, embraced in the weir's shimmering arm-spread, a small island lay anchored, fringed close with willow and silver birch and alder. Reserved, shy, but full of significance, it hid whatever it might hold behind a veil, keeping it till the hour should come, and, with the hour, those who were called and chosen.

Slowly, but with no doubt or hesitation whatever, and in something of a solemn expectancy, the two animals passed through the broken tumultuous water and moored their boat at the flowery margin of the island. In silence they landed, and pushed through the blossom and scented herbage and undergrowth that led up to the level ground, till they stood on a little lawn of a marvellous green, set round with Nature's own orchard-trees – crab-apple, wild cherry, and sloe.

'This is the place of my song-dream, the place the music played to me,' whispered the Rat, as if in a trance. 'Here, in this holy place, here if anywhere, surely we shall find Him!'

Then suddenly the Mole felt a great Awe fall upon him, an awe that turned his muscles to water, bowed his head, and rooted his feet to the ground. It was no panic terror – indeed he felt wonderfully at peace and happy – but it was an awe that smote and held him and, without seeing, he knew it could only mean that some august Presence was very, very near. With difficulty he turned to look for his friend. and saw him at his side cowed, stricken, and trembling violently. And still there was utter silence in the populous bird-haunted branches around them; and still the light grew and grew

Perhaps he would never have dared to raise his eyes, but that, though the piping was now hushed, the call and the summons seemed still dominant and imperious. He might not refuse, were Death himself waiting to strike him instantly, once he had looked with mortal eye on things rightly kept hidden. Trembling he obeyed, and raised his humble head; and then, in that utter clearness of the imminent dawn, while Nature, flushed with fullness of incredible colour, seemed to hold her breath for the event, he looked in the very eyes of the Friend and Helper; saw the backward sweep of the curved horns, gleaming in the growing daylight; saw the stern, hooked nose between the kindly eyes that were looking down on them humorously, while the bearded mouth broke into a half-smile at the corners; saw the rippling muscles on the arm that lay across the broad chest, the long supple hand still holding the pan-pipes only just fallen away from the parted lips; saw the splendid curves of the shaggy limbs disposed in majestic ease on the sward; saw, last of all, nestling between his very hooves, sleeping soundly in entire peace and contentment, the little, round, podgy, childish form of the baby otter. All this he saw, for one moment breathless and intense, vivid on the morning sky; and still, as he looked, he lived; and still, as he lived, he wondered.

'Rat!' he found breath to whisper, shaking. 'Are you afraid?'

'Afraid?' murmured the Rat, his eyes shining with unutterable love. 'Afraid! Of him? O, never, never! And yet – and yet – O, Mole, I am afraid!'

Then the two animals, crouching to the earth, bowed their heads and did worship.

Sudden and magnificent, the sun's broad golden disc showed itself over the horizon facing them; and the first rays, shooting across the level water-meadows, took the animals full in the eyes and dazzled them. When they were able to look once more, the Vision had vanished, and the air was full of the carol of birds that hailed the dawn.

As they stared blankly. in dumb misery deepening as they slowly realised all they had seen and all they had lost, a capricious little breeze, dancing up from the surface of the water, tossed the aspens, shook the dewy roses and blew lightly and caressingly in their faces; and with its soft touch came instant oblivion. For this is the last best gift that the kindly demi- god is careful to bestow on those to whom he has revealed himself in their helping: the gift of forgetfulness. Lest the awful remembrance should remain and grow, and overshadow mirth and pleasure, and the great haunting memory should spoil all the after-lives of little animals helped out of difficulties, in order that they should be happy and lighthearted as before.

Mole rubbed his eyes and stared at Rat, who was looking about him in a puzzled sort of way. 'I beg your pardon; what did you say, Rat?' he asked.

'I think I was only remarking,' said Rat slowly, 'that this was the right sort of place, and that here, if anywhere, we should find him. And look! Why, there he is, the little fellow!' And with a cry of delight he ran towards the slumbering Portly.

(Kenneth Grahame, *The Wind in the Willows*)

**Questions**

1. How far does the experience described here match the religious experiences defined by Rudolf Otto or William James?

2. Who is 'the piper at the gates of Dawn'? To what extent does the description given here correspond to Christian belief? Does it correspond better to another belief system?

2. Why does Rat underplay his experience at the end of this extract?

3. How might a sceptic explain the experience of Rat and Mole?

# Internet research: Medjugorje

Use the Internet to research reports of religious experience, and messages from the Virgin Mary, in Medjugorje. ( www.medjugorje.org is a good place to start).

1. Make brief notes outlining the main details of what is said to have happened at Medjugorje. Include: when and where these visions have happened. Who has received them? What has been the main content of the messages?

2. What can you find out about the recipients of these visions? Did they become Roman Catholics after receiving the messages, or was this already their faith?

3. Which is closest to your own opinion:

(a) these people have genuinely seen and heard the Virgin Mary as an objective reality (it is a **veridical** experience)

(b) these people genuinely believe that they have seen and heard the Virgin Mary, who seems real to them (a **subjectivist** view)

(c) these people are inventing these visions in order to gain attention and publicity (a **sceptical** view), or

(d) a different view?

Try to explain your own responses to the visions at Medjugorje, giving reasons for your interpretation.

# Presentation activity: examples of religious experience

Choose one of the following characters to research. Using books and the Internet (making sure that the sites you use are reputable, and are acknowledged in your work), prepare a presentation for the class of about ten minutes' duration. You might want to make a bullet-pointed handout for your fellow students to keep.

- Julian of Norwich
- the prophet Muhammad (the Night Journey)
- Bernadette Soubirous
- Guru Nanak
- Charles Wesley
- Teresa of Avila
- the Buddha (Enlightenment stories)
- Ramakrishna Paramahamsa
- St Francis of Assisi
- Joan of Arc

**In your presentation, explain:**

- What was the cultural and religious background of this person (for example, when did he or she live and what did he or she believe before the experience)?
- What were the key features of this person's religious experience (for example, voices, visions, gradual understanding, dramatic conversion)?
- How far does the experience fit in with Rudolf Otto's description of religious experience?
- Does the experience pass William James' 'test' of having a lasting value?
- How might a sceptic interpret the experience?

Give your own assessment of whether the experience could be counted as evidence for the existence of God, and be prepared to take questions from the rest of the group and to defend your views.

# Internet research: The Toronto blessing

Search the Internet to find out about the Toronto blessing – you might want to start with Wikipedia, or look at sites produced by the Toronto Airport Christian Fellowship or those which attack it.

1. Find out what the 'Toronto blessing' is – when did it start, and what are its features?

2. What reasons do its supporters give for claiming that this 'blessing' is genuinely from God?

3. What criticisms have been made against the Toronto blessing from those within the Christian church?

4. How might a non-Christian argue against a claim that the Toronto blessing is evidence of the work of the Holy Spirit?

5. How does the Toronto blessing stand up to 'tests' of religious experience such as those suggested by William James or in Galatians?

# Religious experience: examples

Fill in the chart with as many examples as you can find – use them to illustrate the points you make in your essays.

| | |
|---|---|
| **People who claimed to see visions** | **Corporate religious experiences** |
| **People who claimed to hear voices** | **People who claimed to experience miracles** |
| **People who had dramatic conversion experiences** | **People who had a quiet 'inner conviction' of God's presence** |

# Religious experience: revision test questions

1. Who wrote a book called *On Religion, Speeches to its Cultured Despisers*, in which he argued that religious experience was at the essence of religious faith?

2. Which study in 1990 concluded that between half and two-thirds of the adult population claim to have had some kind of religious experience?

3. If a religious experience is described as 'veridical', what does this mean?

4. Who wrote about that we should adopt the 'principle of credulity' when we hear reports of religious experience?

5. What did J. L. Mackie say about the principles of credulity and testimony, in *The Miracle of Theism*?

6. Who, according to the Old Testament, had a vision of God in the Temple, when God touched his mouth with a burning coal?

7. Who argued that a religious experience can be tested by the lasting effect it has on the individual?

8. Who would not believe the experience of the disciples, that they had seen the risen Christ, unless he saw Christ for himself and touched his wounds?

9. Who said that a religious experience was the result of an individual making contact with the archetype of God in the collective unconscious?

10. Who described religious experience as a sense of the 'numinous', combining holiness and dread, in his book *The Idea of the Holy*?

# Religious experience: revision test answers

1. Friedrich Schleiermacher

2. *Religious Experience Today: Studying the Facts* by David Hay – the Hay Report

3. It means it is a real experience of some objective reality.

4. Richard Swinburne

5. He said that it's always going to be more likely that the person is deceiving you, or mistaken, than that the supernatural explanation is the right one. He was following Hume in saying this.

6. The prophet Isaiah

7. William James (and others)

8. 'Doubting' Thomas

9. C. J. Jung

10. Rudolf Otto

# Religious experience: key vocabulary revision sheet

**Credulity** – willingness to believe.

**Ineffable** – difficult or impossible to express adequately in words.

**Monism** – the belief that everything has an essential unity.

**Noetic** – giving knowledge or insight.

**Numinous** – a word created by Rudolf Otto, to mean the 'wholly other'.

**Objectivist view** – the view that if a religious experience truly happens, it demonstrates the existence of a God 'out there'.

**Passivity** – being the object something happens to, rather than the active subject.

**Pragmatism** – pragmatism is a way of thinking which says that the truth or meaning of something depends, at least in part, on its practical consequences.

**Subjectivist view** – the view that religious experience can be true for the believer.

**Transient** – impermanent; not lasting long.

**Veridical** – if an experience is described as veridical, it means that it is a genuine experience of something that is actually there.

# Religious experience: key points revision sheet

- Religious experience is a central part of many religious traditions.

- William James argued, in *The Varieties of Religious Experience*, that the validity of a religious experience could be tested by its results in the life of the person who had the experience.

- James gave religious experience four characteristics:
  1. Ineffability (can't describe it adequately)
  2. Transiency (doesn't last long)
  3. Noetic quality (gives a sense of insight and knowledge)
  4. Passivity (the person having the experience has the sense of being controlled rather than being in control).

- Richard Swinburne argued that we should believe reports of religious experience unless we have a good reason not to – principles of credulity and testimony.

- J. L. Mackie argued in *The Miracle of Theism* that the natural explanation is always going to be more likely than the supernatural one.

- Freud argued that apparent religious experience was simply the result of neurosis coming from the subconscious unconscious layers of the mind, and it did not relate to anything real.

- Rudolf Otto argued that feelings of mystery, transcendence and awe are at the heart of religious experience.

- Antony Flew and other logical positivists argue that claims to religious experience are meaningless because they cannot be verified using the senses.

- Some argue that experiences of different kinds of Gods in different religious traditions indicate that the experiences come from within the mind. Others say that we should expect God to appear in a recognisable form, which will be different in different cultures.

# Religious experience: assessment for learning

Have a look at the following piece of writing, and also look at the level descriptors Edexcel examiners use when they are judging the quality of your work at A2 level.

1. What do you think would be the right band for the work, for Assessment Objective (AO) 1?

For AO1, the work should demonstrate knowledge and understanding. You are looking for:

- Relevance to the question (not just relevance to the general topic)
- Accuracy
- Detail
- Appropriate examples and references
- Thoroughness

2. What do you think would be the right band for AO2?

For AO2, the work should show evaluative skill. You are looking for:

- Relevance to the question
- Reference to different points of view
- Clearly explained reasoning
- A clear and well-supported conclusion that answers the question

3. Once you have decided on the sort of mark you think this work should get, write some comments advising the student so that he or she knows how to improve. Make sure you include some positive comments, saying what was good, as well as saying what he or she could do better next time.

## Sample student answer for assessment

**'People who claim to have had religious experience should be believed.' Discuss.**

People always disagree on what is meant by religious experience, and what counts as a religious experience. Some may say that religious experience can just be having a sense of beauty in the world, or feeling God's presence while praying. Others would say that religious experience has to involve the senses, we have to hear or see something in order for it to be an experience, and this has to come from a supernatural being such as God. Religious experience can also come in different forms such as miracles (for example the feeding of the five thousand in the Bible), mystical experience (for example St Teresa of Avila), or revelations (such as in Luke 1).

Swinburne argues that 'a powerful rational being who is not a material object' is the source of religious experience. He is an example of a philosopher who believes that religious experience is something serious that should be taken seriously by everyone. He wrote *Is there a God* in response to Dawkins's *The Blind Watchmaker* in order to show that the only person that can tell us the truth about their religious experience is the person that experienced it, as they know what happened. However, others such as Hume said that these people can be mistaken, or hallucinating, or Freud would say that the psychological and social pressure makes the person link the experience to God. However, Brian Davies says that this evidence could mean that in order to have these experiences, the person might have to be in an unusual state. Davies dismisses these arguments completely 'these points are not enough to discredit the view that one can reasonably believe in God on the basis of experience'. Swinburne's Principle of Credulity says that experience is reliable and more likely to be true than false so we should believe it until we have sufficient evidence to do otherwise: 'religious perceptual claims deserve to be taken as seriously as perceptual claims of any other kind'. The Principle of Testimony is very similar and says that most of the time (when not mistaken or deliberately lying) people tell the truth so therefore we should trust them.

Swinburne is arguing in much the same way as Hume, although Hume is arguing the opposite. The natural conclusion for Swinburne is that religious experience is down to God, but for Hume the natural conclusion is that religious experience has nothing to do with a God or a supernatural being. Hume believed that religious experience is beyond the realms of reasonable belief, and that anyone that believes that they have had a religious experience are uneducated and come from 'ignorant and barbarous places and nations' and are therefore not to be trusted. Because we have our past experience to show us what happens in nature, we can deduce that religious experience doesn't and cannot happen because there is no scientific explanation for it. Others say that the 'rules' of nature are not rules at all but what we have observed in past years. However, these days we do not rule out things that we do not yet have explanations for, but we try to find these explanations. Some also say that religious experience is not an act of nature but a revelatory experience, in order for the person to change and learn something.

William James is the most well known writer about religious experience. He did not set out to prove or disprove the existence of a God, but collected evidence from ordinary people about the experiences they have had and whether they had value. He put these religious experiences into his book *The Varieties of Religious Experience*. This writing was very different to any other as James tried to avoid putting his own interpretations down, but allowed the experiences to speak for themselves. The evidence that he presented rejected Freud totally. James did not believe that religious experience was connected to psychological factors or sexual consciousness, but to a supernatural being such as God. He did suggest that people that had religious experiences should be believed if they think that it was a religious experience, and that the real test of an experience is the effect it has on the person involved. Was the person converted, and did this conversion last for the rest of their life? For example in Acts 9, Saul did not believe in a God until he had a religious experience that converted him. He then went on in life teaching others and serving God. James would therefore definitely believe that this type of experience should be believed.

The objectivist view of religious experience is that there is a God and he is an object that can be encountered through experience, and this experience is proof for his existence. However, some say that we have no way of knowing that this object is God. The subjectivist view of religious experience is that the effect the experience has on the believer is the most important thing. For example, if the believer has been physically affected, or has decided to change something in their life. They also believe that the meaning of the religious experience is that given by the believer and therefore should be believed and should be the only explanation for it. However, some say that this view reduces religious experience to the level of a mental state such as a dream, and that it is not consistent of the teachings of the Church, or the Bible.

Therefore, there are many views and arguments for and against the belief in religious experience, and often two theologians will argue in the same way but with opposite views. This shows that in answering this question, the fact of whether the person has an original belief in God or not plays a big part. This is why the view that the person has to come to their own conclusions about their experiences themselves before they can be dismissed, and this is also why James was so popular in his writing, as he did not try to influence others with his beliefs.

# Life after death: personal identity

1. Are you the same person that you were when you were seven? What is it that makes you the same? What makes you different? If you had crayoned on the wall when you were seven and it was only discovered today, would it be fair for you to be punished for it now? If someone committed a war crime 40 years ago, would it be fair for him or her to be punished today?

2. If you were to meet the other people in this class in 30 years from now, how would you know which of you was which (without asking!)? What would be the things that you would expect to be the same about each other? What would you expect to have changed? Supposing one of you had changed dramatically in looks and tastes and behaviour – what would make you think 'It's not actually him/her at all' rather than 'what a huge change in him/her'?

3. Is someone who has undergone significant physical changes still the same person (e.g. someone pre- and post-plastic surgery, or someone before and after a sex-change operation, or someone before and after a disfiguring accident)? How would you know it was the same person?

4. Is someone who has suffered a total memory loss, perhaps through trauma or Alzheimer's, still the same person? If that person had committed a crime before the memory loss, should he or she be punished for it later even if there was no recollection of the crime?

5. Is someone who suffers both physical and mental changes still the same person – for example, someone who is confined to a wheelchair and brain damaged by an accident, so that the body is changed, the memory is impaired and the personality is altered? What is it that makes him or her the same, if anything?

6. Suppose human cloning were possible, and scientists created a replica of you, with your exact DNA reproduced in another human being. Would you and the clone be the same person? Why or why not? What if you died the day before the clone came into being – would it make a difference?

7. Imagine someone who has been a recipient of organ donation in every possible way – skin grafts, face transplant, new heart and lungs, new corneas, new kidneys … person A had received the organs, and person B was the donor. Is person A still person A? What if a brain transplant were possible, and person A had person B's brain?

8. People suggest that person C is actually the reincarnation of person D, who died 200 years ago. What would persons C and D have to have in common, for you to be persuaded that person C was in fact person D?

9. Person E dies. What aspects of person E must continue to exist, in order for it to be true to say there is life after death?

# Mind and body

Fill in the boxes with your own ideas and then discuss them with the rest of the group.

| | |
|---|---|
| How, if at all, can I know that other people have minds? | If we have genuine free will to make decisions and choices, does this mean that the mind has to be more than just physical chemical processes? |
| Is it possible to make a mistake about your own mind – for example to think that you believe something when really, you don't? | Would it be possible to make a computer that could genuinely think by itself? How could we tell if it really had a mind of its own? |

# Religion and science: revision test questions

1. What is meant by the word 'hypothesis' in the context of science?

2. What is the name given to the belief that knowledge can best be gained through the experience of the five senses?

3. What is the name given to the theory that the universe began in a massive explosion of matter, energy and heat?

4. What is the position of the scientist Peter Atkins on questions of whether God created the universe?

5. Whose study of geology and fossils led to the uniformitarian theory that the earth was much older than the Bible suggests?

6. What is the name given to the theory that species with advantageous characteristics reproduce more easily, so that over time a species can change to suit its environment?

7. There was a famous debate in Oxford in 1860 in which Darwin's ideas were discussed. Samuel Wilberforce represented the established church – who represented Darwin?

8. What was the Scopes trial and what was the verdict?

9. Who wrote books called *The Genesis Flood* and *Biblical Creationism*, in which he supported a literal understanding of the Bible's version of creation?

10. What is the name of Michael Behe's book, in which he argues that God must have designed creation because of its 'irreducible complexity'?

# Religion and science: revision test answers

1. It is an idea a scientist might have to explain things he or she has observed; experiments test the hypothesis to see if it seems to be the right explanation.

2. Empiricism

3. The Big Bang Theory

4. Atkins takes an atheist position and argues that religious explanations are unnecessary and unscientific.

5. Sir Charles Lyell

6. Evolution (through natural selection)

7. Thomas Huxley

8. It was the trial of John Scopes who was taken to court in Tennessee, USA for teaching evolutionary theory in school. He was found guilty.

9. Henry Morris

10. 'Darwin's Black Box'

# Religion and science: Peter Atkins, 'Awesome versus adipose'

Science is almost totally incompatible with religion. I say "almost," but I do not wish that weasel word to be construed as weakness. The only point of compatibility is that there are well-meaning, honest people on both sides who are genuinely and deeply concerned with discovering the truth about this wonderful world. That having been said, there is no actual compatibility between science and religion.

Science's dispassionate stare examines issues publicly, exchanges information openly, discusses awkward points objectively, and builds up a network of interdependent ideas and theories that progressively expose the complex as an outcome of the simple. Religion's inwardly directed sentimental glow reflects on issues privately, exchanges information by assurance and assertion, discusses awkward points by warfare, terror, and coercion, and builds up a network of conflicting ideas that conceal ignorance under a cloak of high-flown yet empty prose.

Science reveals where religion conceals. Where religion purports to explain, it actually resorts to tautology. To assert that "God did it" is no more than an admission of ignorance dressed deceitfully as an explanation. Science, with its publicly accessible corpus of information and its open, scrutable arguments, can lead the wondering to an understanding of the entire physical world. (Below, of course, I shall have to argue that that is the entire world.)

Science respects the power of the human intellect; religion belittles it. Science gives us the prospect of full understanding, for it continues to show that, given time, there is no aspect of the world that is closed to its scrutiny and explanation. Religion disarmingly avers that human brains are too puny to achieve full comprehension. Yet science is progressively advancing toward complete knowledge, leaving religions bobbing about in its wake.

Science is hard work, but the answers it hews from the rock face of ignorance are reliable. Religion is armchair speculation well fitted to adipose brains. Science cannot answer deep questions by words alone: it draws on the perspiration of countless experimenters and the struggles of theoreticians to make sense of the data. Religion can speculate wildly, and therefore uselessly, from flabby, personal opinion and never be put to the test, except perhaps beyond the grave. There is, of course, no beyond the grave except in the minds of those who cannot come to terms with the prospect of their own annihilation.

Science searches for the underlying simplicity from which springs the astounding complexity that surrounds and delights us. Science is quarrying observations and seeking the ultimate simplicity of existence. Ultimate truth will be of awesome simplicity; tracing that simplicity up into the world of phenomena may well prove to be more demanding than the exposure of the simplicity. But that difficulty will not mean that the discovery of the simplicity is a false foundation. Religion searches for the all-embracing complexity – God – that somehow, and in an intrinsically inscrutable way, accounts for all that there is. The explanation of a lesser entity in terms of a greater one is a perversion of what it means to explain.

But the crux of the argument is not wholly the superiority of science as a mode of understanding the physical world: it is whether that physical world is the entire world, and whether there is any aspect of existence that necessarily lies outside the kingdom of science. If there is, then science cannot claim to be anything more than a partial contributor to global understanding. If there is not, then science is at least potentially capable of providing complete understanding of all there is.

Here, though, we must be very careful to distinguish between questions that have been invented and questions that at least seem to be real. Only the latter are likely to lead to true understanding of the world; the former merely expose the psychological condition of individuals and societies who invent them. I am afraid that, in my view, most of the questions that so exercise the religious are of the former, empty kind. Thus, whereas it may seem to be a perfectly legitimate question to ask, 'What is the purpose of this universe?', in fact that question is a transposition from everyday life. There is no need for this universe to have a purpose: it could be a wholly purposeless accidental entity.

Because religion implicitly asserts that science cannot divine the purpose of the universe, the religious conclude that science's orb is incomplete. That, of course is illogical, for religion cannot be allowed to invent illusory hoops for its adversaries to leap through: hoops, yes; illusory hoops, no. There are several examples of the invention of such hoops, including life after death (not a jot of evidence, if wishful thinking is excluded), the soul (ditto), and the existence of evil in a world created by an infinitely loving God (a trivial problem if there is no such God).

Somewhere on the borderline between the invented and the real lies the question of the human spirit and its associated qualities, such as love and aesthetic appreciation. I grant that these qualities, or at least their physiological appurtenances, exist. The question, then, is whether science can elucidate them.

There is no evidence that it cannot, and it is not unreasonable to suppose that it can without resorting to supernatural importations. Love is a complex emotion, involving genetically controlled responses, hormonal excretions, and intellectual reflections and considerations. Science can elucidate such a condition, even though it will probably never purport to be able to predict whether one individual will fall in love with another (although even dating agencies have some success in that field). Mysterious and complex love may be, but it certainly holds open the prospect of elucidation. Aesthetics, too, is not inconceivably comprehensible. Acts of valour, heroism, creativity, grandeur, and criminality all lie within the domain of psychology, and psychology is at least a twig if not a full-blown branch of science. Complex, agreed; unpredictable, maybe; but not closed to science.

(Peter Atkins, 'Awesome versus adipose: Who *really* works hardest to banish ignorance?', *Free Inquiry*, 18, 1998)

**Questions**

1. Atkins argues that 'To assert that "God did it" is no more than an admission of ignorance dressed deceitfully as an explanation.' Do you agree with his assessment? How might a religious believer respond to this claim?

2. Does Atkins, in your view, present a convincing case for his claim that the physical world is all that there is? What arguments does he provide to support this assertion?

3. Some people argue that there are important aspects of human existence that science cannot explain, such as love, appreciation of beauty, or virtue. How does Atkins answer them? Do you find his point of view convincing?

# Creation science: should it be taught in schools?

**In this extract, Rusty Entrekin, a medical technician and a parent of schoolchildren in Georgia, USA, argues that 'creation science' should be taught as a possibility alongside other explanations of the origins of the universe and the origins of life.**

From www.sixdaycreation.com

Many do not want *any* hypothesis of the origin of life that is not naturalistic taught in our public schools. They do not want high school students to be taught to think critically about particles-to-people evolution at all. No doubt, some of these people are motivated by *naturalism* – the belief that there is no supernatural. They believe that only naturalistic theories should be taught because they think that only these are true or rational. But oddly, many scientists who are religious also think that only naturalistic theories should be taught in public schools. Why is this, and are they justified in thinking this way?

There is a philosophy called *methodological naturalism* (MN) that motivates many scientists to exclude anything but naturalistic explanations from science. Sometimes, terms that describe certain philosophical perspectives, even popular ones, are not well known. That is the case with MN. Even many scientists have not heard of this term, and among those who have, many cannot correctly define it. Often, they confuse it with the scientific method, or with other forms of naturalism. But make no mistake. Even though the term that describes it is not well known, this philosophy has a pervasive influence in modern science. Among those who are familiar with the term and understand the meaning of it, vehement arguments are often made for its legitimacy.

... How would naturalists feel if they were pressured to utilise *methodological theism* – to conduct science as if God exists, even though they think He does not?

It seems to me that *agnostic science* is much more reasonable as a common ground. This would be the philosophy that we should conduct science as though the supernatural may *possibly* exist.

... The theistic or agnostic scientist has an advantage over the MN scientist. He is free to choose between theistic and naturalistic explanations, depending on which seems the most reasonable. The MN scientist, on the other hand, has restricted himself to naturalistic explanations, even when they appear to be quite improbable, counter-intuitive, or irrational.

Science bound by MN cannot, and does not invalidate religion. Since it is not able to even consider supernatural causes, it cannot rule them out. To rule them out, an MN scientist must step outside of science into the realm of metaphysics, or he must adopt an agnostic approach that is open to the possibility of the supernatural, at least for the sake of argument.

What about when there is no plausible naturalistic explanation available? Should we hold out forever waiting for one when other philosophical disciplines offer attractive explanations? If we restrict science to methodological naturalism, then scientists can never consider ideas from these disciplines and deem such conjectures 'scientific'.

What if nature is designed and created by a transcendent metaphysical intelligence? What if the evidence in nature actually points to this? Science bound by methodological naturalism must ignore this; it is forever bound to seek naturalistic explanations, no matter how implausible they may be. It is not free to follow the evidence wherever it may lead. Is this healthy? Is this the approach we really want to take into inquiring into the truth? Should the evidence be the determinant of truth, or a presupposition? (from www.sixdaycreation.com/controversy.doc)

**For discussion:**

- Do you think Entrekin is making fair points?
- Conduct a debate: 'This house believes that creation science should be taught in school science lessons'.'

**Write either:**

- An article in response to Entrekin, arguing the case against teaching creation science in schools.

**or:**

- A letter to parents from the headteacher, explaining why you have decided to add creation science to your science curriculum.

# From Stephen Hawking

Where do we come from? How did the universe begin? Why is the universe the way it is? How will it end? All my life, I have been fascinated by the big questions that face us, and have tried to find scientific answers to them. If, like me, you have looked at the stars, and tried to make sense of what you see, you too have started to wonder what makes the universe exist. The questions are clear, and deceptively simple. But the answers have always seemed well beyond our reach. Until now.

The ideas which had grown over two thousand years of observation have had to be radically revised. In less than a hundred years, we have found a new way to think of ourselves. From sitting at the centre of the universe, we now find ourselves orbiting an average-sized sun, which is just one of millions of stars in our own Milky Way galaxy. And our galaxy itself is just one of billions of galaxies, in a universe that is infinite and expanding. But this is far from the end of a long history of inquiry. Huge questions remain to be answered, before we can hope to have a complete picture of the universe we live in.

"I want you to share my excitement at the discoveries, past and present, which have revolutionised the way we think. From the Big Bang to black holes, from dark matter to a possible Big Crunch, our image of the universe today is full of strange sounding ideas, and remarkable truths. The story of how we arrived at this picture is the story of learning to understand what we see.
(from www.stephenjaygould.org/ctrl/archive/hawking_universe)

**Questions**

1. What differences might it make to religious belief, if we are not the centre of the universe but only a minuscule part of it?

2. If 'scientific' answers could be found to the 'big questions' Hawking raises, would this have to mean the end of religious belief?

3. Do answers to questions of 'what makes the universe exist' have to involve reference to God? Give reasons for your answer.

# A2 Essay writing skills

In a homework essay, you can write as much as you like, with as much relevant detail and explanation as you want to; this will help you when you come to revise. In an exam, you have only a limited time to write each essay, and you need to allow several minutes for planning, choosing the best titles and checking what you have written.

**Planning –** In an exam, your essay plan should only be a few brief notes to help you remember what you were going to write and to order the information you plan to use. The plan should not be detailed at all, and should not take more than a few moments to produce. You haven't got time for any more, and the examiner won't pay much attention to it, however brilliant it might be. It's a good idea to plan your entire exam script before you begin to write any essays – then you will be confident, before you begin, that you have a good exam ahead of you, and you will know that you aren't going to be repeating material. So what if the person next to you has already written a side before you begin your first essay? Yours will be better. You should plan an introduction, about five or six paragraphs (each making different points relevant to the question), and a conclusion. If you discover, at the planning stage, that you haven't got enough to say, then you haven't wasted too much time and can choose a different title.

If this is a homework essay, then you might want to make more detailed notes in your plan for your own use as you go through; you won't be handing this in, so you can write as much or as little as you find useful.

**Selection –** Selecting relevant material is a valuable skill. You don't need to include everything you know on an issue. Look carefully at the title, and start by asking yourself: What's my answer? Is the statement I'm being asked to discuss true or false – why? How have I reached my opinion? Then, you can choose material on the basis of what will support your argument. You need to include material that shows you are aware of different points of view, so that you can explain why you find other possible answers unconvincing. But keep closely to the question throughout your essay, for the highest marks.

**Introduction –** Some examiners claim to be able to tell the quality of a script from the opening sentences. It's important that your opening sentences are impressive, therefore. You don't have to say anything wildly brilliant or original, but you do need to make it clear, right from the start, that you are in control of the material and *understand what the question is asking.* If you just look at the general subject matter of a question, and write a general essay on, say, life after death, or the problem of evil, you could probably get a good C if you do it well; but if you want to get an A or a B, you should look at exactly what the question is asking, and show in the introduction that you understand the issues involved. Explain how you understand the question and show that you can see why it is a significant issue. Pick up any key terms and concepts, and show in your introduction that you understand these.

**The body of the essay –** This will obviously depend on the way the question is asked. If you are going to follow a line of argument, it is often a good idea to set up the case you disagree with first, and then knock it down before presenting your own case. But the question usually gives you a clue about the structure of the essay:

- **'To what extent ...', or 'How far ...' questions –** The first two paragraphs could say to *this* extent your statement is true, here is some evidence to support this and some scholars who agree; the next two could say, but beyond *this* point, it isn't true, and here are the weaknesses and the scholars who have pointed them out.

- **Statement or 'Discuss. ...' questions –** These are similar to the ones that begin with 'To what extent'. The statement usually overstates the case, and you say that it's true so far but no further – you *qualify* it. (If you agree with the statement completely, or think that it doesn't go far enough, then you are free to say so.) You could start by explaining the thinking of people who would agree with such a statement, and then point out how other thinkers have disagreed with them, and why.

- **'Assess the strengths and weaknesses of ...' –** You do just that: explain strengths and weaknesses, and weigh up whether the ideas still stand in spite of their weaknesses or whether the weaknesses discredit them. This second part (the assessment) is crucial for a good grade. If the examiner wanted simply a list of strengths and weaknesses, then the question would say so – but it invites critical comment, where you show that you have the ability to evaluate and consider ideas in an academic way.

**Using examples –** Try to use examples, wherever possible, and show evidence of your reading. When you can, put scholars' names to particular points of view. When you revise, try to remember who thinks what. When you are presenting this information in your essay, don't just make a list – 'Swinburne thinks ...', 'Aquinas says ...', but try to use these scholars' views appropriately to support the argument you are setting out. If you can, say whether these views are convincing, or whether they are weak, but try not to give a list of views on its own without any comment or argument.

**Using background information –** It's usually better to include relevant background detail during the course of your argument, rather than starting with a lot of information that may or may not be relevant to the question before you turn your attention to addressing it. Otherwise you leave the examiner wondering when you are going to begin your answer. Make sure that the information you include is actually relevant; an essay on the rights of the handicapped foetus in ethics, for example, would not need any background information about how an abortion is performed, and this sort of information will waste your time as well as giving the impression that you haven't read the question.

**Evaluating –** This is an essential part of your essay, and it should permeate the whole of your answer, not just suddenly appear in your conclusion. When you present a point of view, make a critical judgement about it: 'Freud argued blah blah... but this seems unconvincing because ...' or 'Freud argued blah blah... and this is a very fair point, because ...', and so on.

**Your own opinion –** In your essay, you don't have to claim to hold a different point of view from the one you actually do hold. There are no 'right' or 'wrong' opinions, at least not as far as examining goes. You don't have to claim to be a Christian, or to believe in God, to show that you understand the Christian points of view (and the same applies to other religions). You can knock down the religious viewpoints, if you want to; if you think the existence of evil does disprove the existence of a loving God, you can say this. If you don't agree with the majority of famous scholars, you don't have to. You also don't have to claim to agree with popular opinion.

The important thing is that you support your opinion with reasoned argument, and remember to include your own thoughts and not just set out different sides of the argument while leaving the examiners to draw their own conclusions. If you were asked in conversation 'How fair is the view that Arsenal is a better team than Chelsea?', and you answered 'Some argue in favour of Arsenal whereas others prefer Chelsea', you wouldn't have given an adequate answer. Also, if you have set out different sides of an academic debate but then you conclude with something that implies 'That's what they all say, but my own view is based entirely on vague feelings and beliefs and the debate hasn't influenced my thoughts in any way', then this is less than impressive too.

**Conclusion –** This is where you summarise your answer to the question (not where you look at what the question is really asking for the first time). You've given your answer in the body of the essay, so all you need now is to summarise it. For example: 'In conclusion, therefore, the statement was only partially true'; 'The argument has some validity, but there are serious flaws in it', or 'It ignores some fundamental questions' and so on. You can give your own opinion here, and side with one group of scholars or another. Or you can say that neither case is entirely convincing. But don't let your essay just stop, without a conclusion. Try to avoid saying 'There are lots of opinions and therefore there isn't one right answer'. This sounds really feeble and isn't even necessarily true – lots of opinions could be wrong, and there *could* be one right answer.

**Example –** If you are asked a question about the strengths and weaknesses of X argument for the existence of God, you could say:

Introduction – Although not everyone would agree that it is necessary to be able to prove the existence of God through reason and logic, many Christian theologians have produced different arguments which attempt to give such a proof. X argument has been a popular way for Christian thinkers to attempt to prove God's existence, but although it has several strengths, it has also been criticised for its failure to address some important issues …

Paragraph 1 – what the argument says, and who says it, using as much key vocabulary as accurately as you can;

Paragraph 2 – some strengths of the argument (and who supports it);

Paragraph 3 – your evaluation of those alleged strengths;

Paragraph 4 – some weaknesses (and who points them out);

Paragraph 5 – your evaluation of those alleged weaknesses.

Conclusion – Therefore, although the X argument does have its strengths, there are some serious difficulties with it, and it leaves several important questions unanswered/the particular weakness I have outlined is an insurmountable problem. It could be argued that any argument for the existence of God is bound to be inconclusive; in fact, many people would argue that it is important that questions of belief remain open. They argue that if God could be conclusively proved, this would deal a serious blow to issues of faith and freedom of choice. *(This is only an example. You might think that X argument is very convincing, in which case, say so.)*

This would be a good essay, because it would deal with the question on the paper all the way through; you are asked to look at the strengths and weaknesses, and this is what the essay does, at every stage. Weaker candidates tend only to look at what the question is asking in their concluding paragraph; they seem to have a mental highlighter pen which picks out one or two words from the title, and then they write a general essay that might as well be called 'All I know on that topic'. Your essays are going to show you know what you're doing right from the start.

# Ontological argument: Kant's refutation

We must ask: Is the proposition that this or that thing (which, whatever it may be, is allowed as possible) exists, an analytic or a synthetic proposition? If it is analytic, the assertion of the existence of the thing adds nothing to the thought of the thing; but in that case either the thought, which is in us, is the thing itself, or we have presupposed an existence as belonging to the realm of the possible, and have then, on that pretext, inferred its existence from its internal possibility – which is nothing but a miserable tautology ...

'Being' is obviously not a real predicate; that is, it is not a concept of something which could be added to the concept of a thing. It is merely the positing of a thing, or of certain determinations, as existing in themselves. Logically, it is merely the copula of a judgement.

(Kant, *Critique of Pure Reason*, trans. Norman Kemp Smith, Macmillan, 1929)

**Questions**

1. Explain the differences between analytic and synthetic propositions.

2. What is a 'tautology'?

3. What is a 'predicate'?

4. Is Kant right when he says that existence is not a predicate?

5. Why is Kant's criticism usually considered to be fatal to the ontological argument?

# Ontological argument: can the ontological argument be used to demonstrate the existence of the Devil?

(1) I have a concept of something than which nothing worse can be conceived.
(2) If that 'something' did not actually, or in fact, exist, it would not be 'that than which nothing *worse* could be conceived,' because something could always be conceived to be much worse, viz., something that actually exists.
(3) This 'greatest something' we shall call the Devil.
Therefore the Devil exists.

This second ontological argument, by parity of reason with the first, seems sound, if indeed, the first is. Is it not conceivable that not only do we have an idea of something that is the worst possible thing, but that it would *have* to exist if it truly *were* the worst possible thing? Hence, the very possibility of the Devil implies his actuality, just as the very possibility of God implies his existence. The logic is the same in both cases.
(From David and Marjorie Haight, 'An ontological argument for the Devil', *The Monist*, 54, 1970)

**Questions**

1. Is this a sound argument?

2. Does changing 'God' to 'the Devil' in this way show that the ontological argument does not work? Or does it actually show that the Devil exists? Or neither?

3. Descartes argued that existence is a perfection. Would this mean that the Devil therefore could not possibly exist?

# Ontological argument: revision test questions

1. In which century did Anselm live?

2. How does Anselm define God?

3. Who criticised Anselm's argument by applying it to the notion of a Lost Island?

4. What is meant by 'necessary existence'?

5. What is an analytic proposition?

6. What did the 'fool say in his heart', according to Psalm 53?

7. Who argued that God's existence is not self-evident, but can be demonstrated in Five Ways?

8. Who described God's attributes in terms of 'perfections'?

9. Who criticised the ontological argument by saying that 'existence is not a predicate'?

10. Which modern scholar claimed that God's existence is either impossible or necessary, and it's not impossible?

# Ontological argument: revision test answers

1. 11th

2. 'That than which nothing greater can be conceived.'

3. Gaunilo

4. It means existence which does not depend on anything else.

5. A statement which gives the definition of something.

6. There is no God.

7. Aquinas

8. Descartes

9. Kant

10. Norman Malcolm

# Ontological argument: key vocabulary revision sheet

**Analytic proposition** – a statement that is true by definition.

***A priori* argument** – an argument based on first principles rather than on experience of the world.

**Cartesian** – relating to Descartes and his thought.

**Contingent existence** – existence which depends on other factors to continue, and which can begin and end.

**Deductive argument** – an argument based on reason and logic, where if the premises are true, the conclusion must also be true.

**Necessary existence** – existence which depends on nothing else, which never begins or ends and which applies only to God.

**Ontological** – to do with existence.

**Predicate –** something that is asserted or denied about the subject of a sentence, (such as 'is good' in 'God is good') a characteristic or quality or attribute.

**Synthetic proposition** – a statement that can be verified using sense experience.

# Ontological argument: key points revision sheet

- The ontological argument is an *a priori*, deductive argument.
- It claims that the statement 'God exists' is analytic rather than synthetic.
- Anselm defined God as 'that than which nothing greater can be conceived.' He argued that therefore God must exist because a real God surpasses a God who is only a concept.
- Gaunilo argued that you could see the flaws in Anselm's argument if you substitute the term 'God' with the term 'Lost Island' and then expected to be able to find that island. Anselm responded by saying that the argument only worked for God because other things, like islands, have contingent existence.
- Descartes' version of the argument said that existence is an aspect of God's perfections, a necessary aspect of what makes God God – just as three angles are necessary to the definition of a triangle.
- Kant disagreed on the grounds that 'existence is not a predicate'.
- Norman Malcolm argues that God's existence is either impossible or necessary, because God cannot come in and out of existence, otherwise he wouldn't be God. He must exist either always or never. God's existence is not impossible, therefore it must be necessary. People criticise Malcolm because the argument seems circular – we have to accept that God has necessary existence before we can demonstrate that God has necessary existence.
- Alvin Plantinga's argument argues using modal logic and considering considers different 'possible worlds'. He calls God 'maximally great' and like Malcolm he argues that if God's existence is not logically contradictory, it must be necessary.

# Ontological argument: practice exam question

Students' work should be measured against the Edexcel levels of response for Religious Studies.

**'Ontological arguments for the existence of God have been shown to fail.'**
**To what extent would you agree with this statement?**

AO1

For high marks in AO1, students should aim for relevance, clarity, accuracy and detail. Here, they need to outline different versions of ontological arguments and different criticisms. They should aim to use key vocabulary with accuracy, and should make reference to the thinking of various scholars such as Anselm, Descartes, Plantinga and Kant.

AO2

To achieve a high level, students should make an attempt at critical analysis. They should make reference to alternative different points of viewpoints and use balanced reasoning. Their arguments should be expressed accurately and fluently, and they should use a range of technical vocabulary. They should reach a conclusion which is well supported by the rest of the answer, rather than just tacked on at the end. Here, they need to assess the strength of the ontological argument and strengths of its criticism. They might conclude that Kant's point was fair and that the ontological argument is using tricks with words to move from predication to existence; they might conclude that the ontological argument still does have value, and they could refer to modern versions of the argument (e.g. Malcolm, Plantinga) to indicate that there are still those who support it despite the objections of Kant and others.

# Extract from Sigmund Freud: *The Future of an Illusion*

For the individual, too, life is hard to bear, just as it is for mankind in general. The civilization in which he participates imposes some amount of privation on him, and other men bring him a measure of suffering, either in spite of the precepts of his civilization or because of its imperfections. To this are added the injuries which untamed nature – he calls it Fate – inflicts on him. One might suppose that this condition of things would result in a permanent state of anxious expectation in him and a severe injury to his natural narcissism. ... But how does he defend himself against the superior powers of nature, of Fate, which threaten him as they threaten all the rest?

Civilization relieves him of this task; it performs it in the same way for all alike; and it is noteworthy that in this almost all civilizations act alike. Civilization does not call a halt in the task of defending man against nature, it merely pursues it by other means. The task is a manifold one. Man's self-regard, seriously menaced, calls for consolation; life and the universe must be robbed of their terrors; moreover his curiosity, moved, it is true, by the strongest practical interest, demands an answer. ...

This situation is nothing new. It has an infantile prototype, of which it is in fact only the continuation. For once before one has found oneself in a similar state of helplessness: as a small child, in relation to one's parents. One had reason to fear them, and especially one's father; and yet one was sure of his protection against the dangers one knew. Thus it was natural to assimilate the two situations ... man makes the forces of nature not simply into persons with whom he can associate as he would with his equals – that would not do justice to the overpowering impression which those forces make on him – but he gives them the character of a father. He turns them into gods, following in this, as I have tried to show ...

But man's helplessness remains and along with it his longing for his father, and the gods. The gods retain their threefold task: they must exorcise the terrors of nature, they must reconcile men to the cruelty of Fate, particularly as it is shown in death, and they must compensate them for the sufferings and privations which a civilized life in common has imposed on them.

(Freud, *The Future of an Illusion*, first published 1927, W. W. Norton, 1989)

**Questions**

1. What are the conditions that Freud thinks people try to escape from, and need comfort from?

2. Why do people use the image of their fathers when creating a version of God, according to Freud in this passage?

3. To what extent do you think Freud is right?

# God is dead: Friedrich Nietzsche, The Gay Science

*THE MADMAN* – Have you not heard of that madman who lit a lantern in the bright morning hours, ran to the market place, and cried incessantly: 'I seek God! I seek God!' – As many of those who did not believe in God were standing around just then, he provoked much laughter. Has he got lost? asked one. Did he lose his way like a child? asked another. Or is he hiding? Is he afraid of us? Has he gone on a voyage? Emigrated? – Thus they yelled and laughed.

The madman jumped into their midst and pierced them with his eyes. 'Whither is God?' he cried; 'I will tell you. *We have killed him* – you and I. All of us are his murderers. But how did we do this? How could we drink up the sea? Who gave us the sponge to wipe away the entire horizon? What were we doing when we unchained this earth from its sun? Whither is it moving now? Whither are we moving? Away from all suns? Are we not plunging continually? Backward, sideward, forward, in all directions? Is there still any up or down? Are we not straying, as through an infinite nothing? Do we not feel the breath of empty space? Has it not become colder? Is not night continually closing in on us? Do we not need to light lanterns in the morning? Do we hear nothing as yet of the noise of the gravediggers who are burying God? Do we smell nothing as yet of the divine decomposition? Gods, too, decompose. God is dead. God remains dead. And we have killed him.

'How shall we comfort ourselves, the murderers of all murderers? What was holiest and mightiest of all that the world has yet owned has bled to death under our knives: who will wipe this blood off us? What water is there for us to clean ourselves? What festivals of atonement, what sacred games shall we have to invent? Is not the greatness of this deed too great for us? Must we ourselves not become gods simply to appear worthy of it? There has never been a greater deed; and whoever is born after us – for the sake of this deed he will belong to a higher history than all history hitherto.'

Here the madman fell silent and looked again at his listeners; and they, too, were silent and stared at him in astonishment. At last he threw his lantern on the ground, and it broke into pieces and went out. 'I have come too early,' he said then; 'my time is not yet. This tremendous event is still on its way, still wandering; it has not yet reached the ears of men. Lightning and thunder require time; the light of the stars requires time; deeds, though done, still require time to be seen and heard. This deed is still more distant from them than most distant stars – *and yet they have done it themselves*.

It has been related further that on the same day the madman forced his way into several churches and there struck up his *requiem aeternam deo*. Led out and called to account, he is said always to have replied nothing but: 'What after all are these churches now if they are not the tombs and sepulchres of God?"

(Nietzsche, *The Gay Science*, first published 1882, Vintage, 1974)

# Extract from Bertrand Russell: 'Why I am Not a Christian'

Religion is based, I think, primarily and mainly upon fear. It is partly the terror of the unknown and partly, as I have said, the wish to feel that you have a kind of elder brother who will stand by you in all your troubles and disputes. Fear is the basis of the whole thing – fear of the mysterious, fear of defeat, fear of death. Fear is the parent of cruelty, and therefore it is no wonder if cruelty and religion have gone hand in hand. It is because fear is at the basis of those two things. In this world we can now begin a little to understand things, and a little to master them by help of science, which has forced its way step by step against the Christian religion, against the churches, and against the opposition of all the old precepts. Science can help us to get over this craven fear in which mankind has lived for so many generations. Science can teach us, and I think our own hearts can teach us, no longer to look around for imaginary supports, no longer to invent allies in the sky, but rather to look to our own efforts here below to make this world a better place to live in, instead of the sort of place that the churches in all these centuries have made it.

(1927, reprinted in *Why I am Not a Christian and Other Essays*, Routledge, 2004)

**Questions**

1. When Russell says that religion is based on fear, what sorts of things does he think religious believers are afraid of? Do you think this is a fair assessment?

2. What solution does Russell offer in place of religion? Why does he think it would 'make this world a better place to live in'?

3. How might a religious believer respond to Russell on this point?

# Humanism: Linda Smith talks to Laurie Taylor

**Linda Smith, a comedian, was president of the British Humanist Association (BHA) from 2004 until her death in 2006.**

So what had persuaded her to accept the presidency of the BHA? 'You want to know how it came about? I did this programme on Radio 4 called Devout Sceptics with Bel Mooney. I was just getting over flu at the time and I felt tired. Really tired. I talked about the whole business of the Holocaust and how if God was going to show his face that might have been quite a good time for him to have done it. I mean, was he waiting for something worse to happen before he stepped in? I remember Bel saying that religious people would reply by asking where man had been at the time. But, as I said, at least some humans did help. God did nothing at all. Missed his big chance. And then I went on to say that I thought of God in much the same way that I think of the royal family. If we didn't live in this toytown with princes and kings and so on then we might make a better stab at being citizens.

'Afterwards I thought to myself, "Oh no, I must have been talking complete nonsense".' But it turned out that there was a really big postbag following the programme. So many people writing in to say that it was so good to hear a non-religious view on the radio. Of course, there were one or two who said that I was a sinner and that unless I repented I would burn in hell. The ones that were signed 'Yours in the love of Christ'. Then I got a letter from Hanne at the BHA which took me totally by surprise. She said she'd heard the programme and was pleased to hear my humanist views. Until that moment I'd never thought of categorising my views as humanism. But I came and met Hanne and chatted and realised that was a fair description."

... Was there any religion in the family? 'No, not really. My dad had been brought up a Catholic and lapsed. I went to Sunday school and there was a time round about the age of eight or nine when I was very taken with the romance of it all, with the idea of Jesus and Easter and rising from the dead, but that faded and pop stars and actors took its place. But even then I always went against the herd. I liked David Bowie and not David Cassidy. But it was secondary school, Bexleyheath Comprehensive, that really put me off God. I suddenly thought in assembly that this was all rubbish, all these stupid old gits like the headmaster and the deputy headmaster reading out this piffle and all these sulky kids moving their mouths to these hymns. I do remember enquiring whether or not you could be removed from assembly on the grounds of being an atheist, but I was told that it didn't count. You could only be excluded if you were Jewish, Catholic or Muslim. But not believing in God was not a valid reason.'

(Extract from an interview for the *New Humanist*, 119 (5), October 2004)

# The soul: From Plato's *Phaedo*

**Socrates, in dialogue with Simmias, talks about the distinction between the soul and the body.**

Do we believe that there is such a thing as death?

To be sure, replied Simmias.

And is this anything but the separation of soul and body? And being dead is the attainment of this separation; when the soul exists in herself, and is parted from the body and the body is parted from the soul – that is death?

Exactly: that and nothing else, he replied.

And what do you say of another question, my friend, about which I should like to have your opinion, and the answer to which will probably throw light on our present inquiry: Do you think that the philosopher ought to care about the pleasures – if they are to be called pleasures – of eating and drinking?

Certainly not, answered Simmias.

And what do you say of the pleasures of love – should he care about them?

By no means.

And will he think much of the other ways of indulging the body – for example, the acquisition of costly raiment, or sandals, or other adornments of the body? Instead of caring about them, does he not rather despise anything more than nature needs? What do you say?

I should say the true philosopher would despise them.

Would you not say that he is entirely concerned with the soul and not with the body? He would like, as far as he can, to be quit of the body and turn to the soul.

That is true.

In matters of this sort philosophers, above all other men, may be observed in every sort of way to dissever the soul from the body.

That is true.

Whereas, Simmias, the rest of the world are of opinion that a life which has no bodily pleasures and no part in them is not worth having; but that he who thinks nothing of bodily pleasures is almost as though he were dead.

That is quite true.

What again shall we say of the actual acquirement of knowledge? – is the body, if invited to share in the inquiry, a hinderer or a helper? I mean to say, have sight and hearing any truth in them? Are they not, as the poets are always telling us, inaccurate witnesses? and yet, if even they are inaccurate and indistinct, what is to be said of the other senses? – for you will allow that they are the best of them?

Certainly, he replied.

Then when does the soul attain truth? – for in attempting to consider anything in company with the body she is obviously deceived.

Yes, that is true.

Then must not existence be revealed to her in thought, if at all?

Yes.

And thought is best when the mind is gathered into herself and none of these things trouble her – neither sounds nor sights nor pain nor any pleasure – when she has as little as possible to do with the body, and has no bodily sense or feeling, but is aspiring after being?

That is true.

And in this the philosopher dishonours the body; his soul runs away from the body and desires to be alone and by herself?

That is true.

(*Phaedo* by Plato Cambridge University Press 1993)

# Heaven and hell: discussion questions

**Heaven**

- If there is a heaven, what would you want it to be like?
- Would you want to be able to see what goes on in the world after your death?
- Would you want to have the opportunity to contact the living?
- What would people have to do in their earthly lives to make heaven a fair reward?
- Do you think you would ever get bored with heaven?
- If there is no sorrow in heaven, but some of your friends and family went to hell, how could that work – would you have to stop caring about them?

**Hell**

- If there is a hell, what would you imagine it to be like? Would it have to be the worst place imaginable?
- What would people have to do in their earthly lives to make eternal hell a fair punishment?
- Do you think belief in the existence of hell is compatible with belief in a perfect, loving God?
- Do you think hell might get boring after a while, so that the punishment stopped having any effect?
- What might the point of eternal punishment be?
- Do you think God would know who was going to heaven and who was going to hell, before they were even born?

# Life after death: from 1 Corinthians 15

But if it is preached that Christ has been raised from the dead, how can some of you say that there is no resurrection of the dead? If there is no resurrection of the dead, then not even Christ has been raised. And if Christ has not been raised, our preaching is useless and so is your faith. More than that, we are then found to be false witnesses about God, for we have testified about God that he raised Christ from the dead. But he did not raise him if in fact the dead are not raised. For if the dead are not raised, then Christ has not been raised either. And if Christ has not been raised, your faith is futile; you are still in your sins. Then those also who have fallen asleep in Christ are lost. If only for this life we have hope in Christ, we are to be pitied more than all men. …

Now if there is no resurrection, what will those do who are baptised for the dead? If the dead are not raised at all, why are people baptised for them? And as for us, why do we endanger ourselves every hour? I die every day – I mean that, brothers – just as surely as I glory over you in Christ Jesus our Lord. If I fought wild beasts in Ephesus for merely human reasons, what have I gained? If the dead are not raised, 'Let us eat and drink, for tomorrow we die.' ...

But someone may ask, 'How are the dead raised? With what kind of body will they come?' How foolish! What you sow does not come to life unless it dies. When you sow, you do not plant the body that will be, but just a seed, perhaps of wheat or of something else. But God gives it a body as he has determined, and to each kind of seed he gives its own body. All flesh is not the same: men have one kind of flesh, animals have another, birds another and fish another. There are also heavenly bodies and there are earthly bodies; but the splendour of the heavenly bodies is one kind, and the splendour of the earthly bodies is another. The sun has one kind of splendour, the moon another and the stars another; and star differs from star in splendour. So will it be with the resurrection of the dead. The body that is sown is perishable, it is raised imperishable; it is sown in dishonour, it is raised in glory; it is sown in weakness, it is raised in power; it is sown a natural body, it is raised a spiritual body. If there is a natural body, there is also a spiritual body. ...

The spiritual did not come first, but the natural, and after that the spiritual. The first man was of the dust of the earth, the second man from heaven. As was the earthly man, so are those who are of the earth; and as is the man from heaven, so also are those who are of heaven. And just as we have borne the likeness of the earthly man, so shall we bear the likeness of the man from heaven.

(1 Corinthians 15: 12–19, 29–32, 35–42, 46–9)

**Questions**
1. Why does Paul think that belief in resurrection is essential for Christians?
2. How does Paul answer the question of whether people have bodies after death?
3. What philosophical problems are raised by Paul's understanding of life after death? Is his understanding of resurrection coherent?

# Life after death: What are the criteria for getting into heaven, according to Christianity?

**Look up the following passages, and make a note of:**

1. The main point that is being made in the passage.
2. A key phrase you could use as a quotation.

What are the key features of Christian teaching about who will have eternal life in heaven? Is the teaching consistent?

- Matthew 19:16–30
- Matthew 25:31–46
- Luke 13:22–8
- John 3:16–19
- Romans 10:9–13
- 2 Thessalonians 2:13–14

- Titus 3:3–7
- Romans 10:9–13
- 2 Thessalonians 2:13–14
- Matthew 19:16–30
- Luke 13:22–28
- John 3:16–19
- 1 John 4:17–21

# Life after death: excerpt from a Buddhist sacred text

### Personal identity and rebirth

The king asked: 'When someone is reborn, Venerable Nagasena, is he the same as the one who just died, or is he another?'

The elder replied: 'He is neither the same nor another.'

'Give me an illustration!'

'What do you think, Great King? When you were a tiny infant, newly born and quite soft, were you then the same as the one who is now grown up?'

'No, that infant was one, I, now grown up, am another.'

'If that is so, then, Great King, you have had no mother, no father, no reaching, no schooling! Do we then take it that there is one mother for the embryo in the first stage, another for the second stage, another for the third, another for the fourth, another for the baby, another for the grown-up man? Is the school-boy one person, and the one who has finished school another? Does one commit a crime, but the hands and feet of another are cut off?'

'Certainly not! But what would you say, Reverend Sir, to all that?'

The elder replied: 'I was neither the tiny infant, newly born and quite soft, nor am I now the grown-up man; but all these are comprised in one unit depending on this very body.'

'Give me a simile!'

'If a man were to light a lamp, could it give light throughout the whole night?'

'Yes, it could.'

'Is now the flame which burns in the first watch of the night the same as the one which burns in the second?'

'It is not the same.'

'Or is the flame which burns in the second watch the same as the one which burns in the last one?'

'It is not the same.'

'Do we then take it that there is one lamp in the first watch of the night, another in the second, and another again in the third?'

'No, it is just because of the light of the lamp shines throughout the night.'

'Even so must we understand the collocation of a series of successive dharmas. At rebirth one dharma arises, while another stops; but the two processes take place almost simultaneously (i.e. they are continuous). Therefore, the first act of consciousness in the new existence is neither the same as the last act of consciousness in the previous existence, nor it is the another.'

'Give me another simile!'

'Milk, once the milking is done, turns after sometimes into curds; from curds it turns into fresh butter; and from fresh butter into ghee. Would it now be correct to say that the milk is the same thing as the curds, or the fresh butter, or the ghee?'

'No, it would not. But they have been produced because of it.'

'Just so must be understood the collocation of a series of successive dharmas.'

**Personal identity and karma**

The king asked: 'Is there, Venerable Nagasena, any being which passes on from this body to another body?'

'No, Your Majesty!'

'If there were no passing on from this body to another, would not one then in one's next life be freed from the evil deeds committed in the past?'

'Yes, that would be so if one were not linked once again with a new organism. But since, Your Majesty, one is linked once again with a new organism, therefore one is not freed from one's evil deeds.'

'Give me a simile!'

'If a man should steal another man's mangoes, would he deserve a thrashing for that?'

'Yes, of course!'

'But he would not have stolen the very same mangoes as the other one had planted. Why should he deserve a thrashing?'

'For the reason that the stolen mangoes had grown because of those that were planted.'

'Just so, Your Majesty, it is because of the deeds one does, whether pure or impure, by means of this psycho-physical organism, that one is once again linked with another psycho-physical organism, and is not freed from one's evil deeds.'

'Very good, Venerable Nagasena!'

The king said: 'Is it through wise attention that people become exempt from further rebirth?'

'Yes, that is due to wise attention, and also to wisdom, and the other wholesome dharmas.'

'But is not wise attention the same as wisdom?'

'No, Your Majesty! Attention is one thing, and wisdom another. Sheep and goats, oxen and buffaloes, camels and asses have attention, but wisdom they have not.'

'Well put, Venerable Nagasena!'

(from *The Questions of King Milinda* see www.buddhanet.net)

# The soul and life after death: revision test questions

1. What are the three different elements of the soul, according to Plato?

2. What is the name given to the belief that we are no more than physical creatures?

3. Which philosopher of religion developed a 'replica theory' about life after death?

4. Who wrote a book called *Twenty Cases Suggestive of Reincarnation*?

5. What is the soul, or 'essential Self', known as in Hindu thought?

6. Who said 'Life is just bytes and bytes and bytes of digital information'?

7. Who wrote a book called *Defending the Soul*?

8. Who argued that plants have 'nutritive' souls and animals have 'perceptive' souls?

9. Which religion teaches that there will be a Messianic age when the dead will be raised from their graves?

10. In which letter does Paul write about the difference between physical bodies and spiritual bodies?

11. Name a moral philosopher who thought that eternal heaven would become boring.

12. Who wrote 'Survival and the Idea of Another World', in which he suggested that disembodied existence is a coherent concept?

# The soul and life after death: revision test answers

1. Reason, emotion, appetite

2. Materialism

3. John Hick

4. Ian Stevenson

5. Atman

6. Richard Dawkins

7. Keith Ward

8. Aristotle

9. Judaism

10. 1 Corinthians

11. Bernard Williams – or another acceptable answer

12. H. H. Price

# The soul and life after death: key vocabulary and key points revision sheet

**Anatta** – the Buddhist belief that there is no essential Self.

**Atman** – the 'essential Self' in Hindu thought.

**Disembodied or discarnate existence** – existence as consciousness but without a physical body.

**Dualism** – the belief in two separate worlds or entities, such as a belief in a distinction between body and soul, or between God and the Devil.

**Karma** – the eternal law by which people experience the consequences of their actions, whether good or bad.

**Reincarnation** – rebirth into a new physical body on this earth after death. This is the teaching of Hinduism, Buddhism and Sikhism.

**Resurrection** – being brought back to life after death, in a new physical form in a different world. This is the belief of many Christians and Muslims, and some Jews.

- Antony Flew argued that the whole discussion of life after death is meaningless because they are mutually exclusive states.
- Kant believed that we have to postulate the existence of life after death in order to reach the '*summum bonum*'.
- Keith Ward and Richard Swinburne defend the existence of the soul from a Christian perspective.
- Ian Stevenson's study of *Twenty Cases Suggestive of Reincarnation* led him to the conclusion that memories of past lives are well authenticated and could be evidence of reincarnation.
- Bernard Williams believed that life in heaven would become boring and pointless.
- John Hick argued that it is not inconceivable that our bodies could be replicated in heaven. He argued that a God of love would save everybody, so the afterlife is an opportunity to continue to develop into our full potential. Hick's critics argue that this denies free will and makes the life and death of Jesus insignificant.
- H. H. Price suggested that disembodied existence is a coherent concept if we imagine a world made of our own mental images, memories and desires. Others criticise him on the grounds that this is inconsistent with religious teaching.
- Some (such as Kenneth Ring) argue that near death experiences provide evidence for life after death, while others (such as Susan Blackmore) argue that the evidence they provide is flimsy and can be artificially recreated.

# The soul and life after death: practice exam question

Students' work should be marked in conjunction with Edexcel's levels of response for A2.

**'The concept of disembodied existence after death is incoherent.' Discuss.**

AO1

For high marks in AO1, candidates should choose information relevant to the title rather than attempting to include everything they know. Here, although they might want to mention other views about life after death, such as resurrection and reincarnation, they should not spend much time on them but should focus clearly on the question and the idea of disembodied existence. They could make useful reference to thinkers such as Price and Swinburne, and should aim to support their answer with examples and quotations where appropriate.

AO2

In evaluation for this question, candidates need to consider whether it makes any sense to speak of disembodied existence after death. They might wish to consider the views of those who claim that any kind of life after death is an incoherent concept because life and death are mutually exclusive states; they could include the views of Flew and Dawkins. They could evaluate the suggestions put forward by Price and discuss whether this is a coherent suggestion.

For high marks in AO2, candidates should try to sustain a line of argument throughout the essay, rather than simply tagging on an unsupported opinion at the end of a long passage of description. When they present the views of different thinkers, they should aim to give some critical comment of on those thinkers' views, rather than simply describing them. Outlining a range of different perspectives is description, not evaluation – for high marks in AO2, candidates need to make critical comment by pointing out strengths or weaknesses in different points of view and showing why they are more persuaded by one argument than by another. They should have a clear conclusion.

# Religious language: discussion starter activity

Photocopy the following page onto card, and cut it into two separate pictures. (The card or paper must be thick enough for it to be impossible to see what's on the picture through the back of the card.)

Everyone needs to be equipped with paper and pen or pencil.

Invite one student to the front of the class and give him or her Picture A to hold so that the rest of the class can't see the picture. The student must describe the picture to the other students in the group, and they have to draw it based on the description. Afterwards, compare the results to see how closely their pictures match the one on card A.

The person with the best attempt at Picture A changes places with the student at the front, and is given Picture B. The students attempt the same task again, drawing from a description provided by this second student.

**Discussion:**

- Why was it so much more difficult to describe and draw Picture B, than Picture A?

  With a little luck, the students will make some of the following points:

- Picture A was of something that they could recognise, whereas Picture B bore no relation to anything in their experience. Picture A enabled the use of commonly understood terms such as 'straight line', 'right angle', 'square', whereas the possibility of using these terms for Picture B was limited.

- Perhaps the student describing Picture B might have used some analogies, (e.g. 'it's a little bit like a snail', 'it looks like smoke'). What sort of analogies did he or she choose? Were they helpful or misleading?

- Could it have been possible for Picture B to be described in such a way that the listeners understood exactly what to draw? How might the description have been improved?

- What difficulties do religious believers face when they are trying to use language to convey ideas such as 'God', 'the soul', 'salvation'?
- How might religious believers communicate their ideas to others in an effective way? –
- What strategies might they employ?
- Is it possible for religious believers to convey their meaning in such a way that other people will know exactly what they mean?

**Picture A**

**Picture B**

# Very Like a Whale by Ogden Nash

One thing that literature would be greatly the better for
Would be a more restricted employment by authors of simile and metaphor.
Authors of all races, be they Greeks, Romans, Teutons or Celts,
Can't seem just to say that anything is the thing it is but have to go out of their way to say that it is like something else.
What does it mean when we are told
That the Assyrian came down like a wolf on the fold?
In the first place, George Gordon Byron had had enough experience
To know that it probably wasn't just one Assyrian, it was a lot of Assyrians.
However, as too many arguments are apt to induce apoplexy and thus hinder longevity,
We'll let it pass as one Assyrian for the sake of brevity.
Now then, this particular Assyrian, the one whose cohorts were gleaming in purple and gold,
Just what does the poet mean when he says he came down like a wolf on the fold?
In heaven and earth more than is dreamed of in our philosophy there are a great many things,
But I don't imagine that among them there is a wolf with purple and gold cohorts or purple and gold anythings.
No, no, Lord Byron, before I'll believe that this Assyrian was actually like a wolf I must have some kind of proof;
Did he run on all fours and did he have a hairy tail and a big red mouth and big white teeth and did he say Woof woof?
Frankly I think it very unlikely, and all you were entitled to say, at the very most,
Was that the Assyrian cohorts came down like a lot of Assyrian cohorts about to destroy the Hebrew host.
But that wasn't fancy enough for Lord Byron, oh dear me no, he had to invent a lot of figures of speech and then interpolate them,
With the result that whenever you mention Old Testament soldiers to people they say Oh yes, they're the ones that a lot of wolves dressed up in gold and purple ate them.
That's the kind of thing that's being done all the time by poets, from Homer to Tennyson;
They're always comparing ladies to lilies and veal to venison,
And they always say things like that the snow is a white blanket after a winter storm.
Oh it is, is it, all right then, you sleep under a six-inch blanket of snow and I'll sleep under a half-inch blanket of unpoetical blanket material and we'll see which one keeps warm,
And after that maybe you'll begin to comprehend dimly,
What I mean by too much metaphor and simile.

('Very Like a Whale' from *The Best of Ogden Nash* by Ogden Nash, Ivan R. Dee Inc 2007)

# Religious language: 'Theology and Falsification', Antony Flew

Let us begin with a parable. It is a parable developed from a tale told by John Wisdom in his haunting and revelatory article 'Gods'. Once upon a time two explorers came upon a clearing in the jungle. In the clearing were growing many flowers and many weeds. One explorer says, 'some Some gardener must tend this plot'. The other disagrees, 'There is no gardener'. So they pitch their tents and set a watch. No gardener is ever seen. 'But perhaps he is an invisible gardener.' So they, set up a barbed-wire fence. They electrify it. They patrol with bloodhounds. (For they remember how H. G. Wells's *The Invisible Man* could be both smelt and touched though he could not be seen.) But no shrieks ever suggest that some intruder has received a shock. No movements of the wire ever betray an invisible climber. The bloodhounds never give cry. Yet still the Believer is not convinced. 'But there is a gardener, invisible, intangible, insensible to electric shocks, a gardener who has no scent and makes no sound, a gardener who comes secretly to look after the garden which he loves.' At last the Sceptic despairs, 'But what remains of your original assertion? Just how does what you call an invisible, intangible, eternally elusive gardener differ from an imaginary gardener or even from no gardener at all?'

In this parable we can see how what starts as an assertion that something exists or that there is some analogy between certain complexes of phenomena, may be reduced step by step to an altogether different status, to an expression perhaps of a 'picture preference'. The Sceptic says there is no gardener. The Believer says there is a gardener (but invisible, etc.). One man talks about sexual behaviour. Another man prefers to talk of Aphrodite (but knows that there is not really a superhuman person additional to, and somehow responsible for, all sexual phenomena). The process of qualification may be checked at any point before the original assertion is completely withdrawn and something of that first assertion will remain (tautology). Mr. Wells's invisible man could not, admittedly, be seen, but in all other respects he was a man like the rest of us. But though the process of qualification may be, and of course usually is, checked in time, it is not always judiciously so halted. Someone may dissipate his assertion completely without noticing that he has done so. A fine brash hypothesis may thus be killed by inches, the death by a thousand qualifications.

And in this, it seems to me, lies the peculiar danger, the endemic evil, of theological utterance. Take such utterances as 'God has a plan', 'God created the world', 'God loves us as a father loves his children'. They look at first sight very much like assertions, vast cosmological assertions. Of course, this is no sure sign that they either are, or are intended to be assertions. But let us confine ourselves to the cases where those who utter such sentences intend them to express assertions. (Merely remarking parenthetically, that those who intend or interpret such utterances as crypto-commands, expressions of wishes, disguised ejaculations, concealed ethics, or as anything else but assertions, are unlikely to succeed in making them either properly orthodox or practically effective.)

Now to assert that such and such is the case is necessarily equivalent to denying that such and such is not the case. Suppose then that we are in doubt as to what someone who gives vent to an utterance is asserting, or suppose that, more radically, we are sceptical as to whether he is really asserting anything at all, one way of trying to understand (or perhaps it will be to expose) his utterance is to attempt to find what he would regard as counting against, or as being incompatible with, its truth. For if the utterance is indeed an assertion, it will necessarily be equivalent to a denial of the negation of that assertion. And anything which would count against the assertion, or which would induce the speaker to withdraw it and to admit that it had been mistaken, must be part of (or the whole of) the meaning of the negation of that assertion. And to know the meaning of the negation of an assertion, is near as makes no matter, to know the meaning of that assertion. And if there is nothing which a putative assertion denies then there is nothing which it asserts either; and so it is not really an assertion. When the Sceptic in the parable asked the Believer, 'Just how does what you call an invisible, intangible, eternally elusive gardener differ from an imaginary gardener or even from no gardener at all?' he was suggesting that the Believer's earlier statement had been so eroded by qualification that it was no longer an assertion at all.

Now it often seems to people who are not religious as if there was no conceivable event or series of events the occurrence of which would be admitted by sophisticated religious people to be a sufficient reason for conceding 'There wasn't a God after all' or 'God does not really love us then'. Someone tells us that God loves us as a father loves his children. We are reassured. But then we see a child dying of inoperable cancer of the throat. His earthly father is driven frantic in his efforts to help, but his Heavenly Father reveals no obvious sign of concern. Some qualification is made – God's love is 'not a merely human love' or it is 'an inscrutable love', perhaps – and we realise that such sufferings are quite compatible with the truth of the assertion that 'God loves us as a father (but, of course, ...)'. We are reassured again. But then perhaps we ask: what is this assurance of God's (appropriately qualified) love worth, what is this apparent guarantee really a guarantee against? Just what would have to happen not merely (morally and wrongly) to tempt but also (logically and rightly) to entitle us to say 'God does not love us' or even 'God does not exist'? I therefore put to the succeeding sym-posiasts... the simple central question, 'What would have to occur or to have occurred to constitute for you a disproof of the love of, or of the existence of, God?'

(Antony Flew, 'Theology and Falsification', 1950, in A. Flew and A. MacIntyre, *New Essays in Philosophical Theology*, SCM Press, 1955)

**Questions**

1. What does Flew mean, when he writes of a 'death by a thousand qualifications'?

2. Flew's parable asks: 'Just how does what you call an invisible, intangible, eternally elusive gardener differ from an imaginary gardener or even from no gardener at all?' How *does* an invisible, intangible God differ from an imaginary God, or from no God at all?

3. How might a theist answer the question with which Flew ends his article?

4. Do you think Flew is right? Why, or why not?

# Religious language: *the via negativa*

**'Face to faith'**

**God is only apprehended when words at last fall silent, says Mark Vernon.**

**Saturday November 25, 2006**
**The *Guardian***
Something remarkable happened on St Nicholas's Day, December 6, 1273. Saint Thomas Aquinas, the theological genius of the medieval period – a man who had set down millions of words on matters in nature and logic, in metaphysics and morality – abruptly put down his pen. He did not write again. When begged to continue, he replied he could not because 'all I have written seems like straw'.

The reference to straw did not mean his output suddenly seemed worthless to him. Rather, straw was a metaphor for basics: like the crude material used for building a house, his words now seemed like rough stuff. His goal had been to understand God. He had made many verbal attempts on the summit. But while his efforts had produced wonderful reflections he had reached the point where he was able to appreciate the most profound truth – the peak lies beyond. God is unknown. His silence was not a rejection but the culmination of his work.

Today, it seems, many believers forget that the first and last thing that can and should be said about God is that God is unknown. Consider the kind of evangelical religiosity in which worship ceases to be an encounter with the mystery of God and becomes instead a feelgood experience, a time for sharing with a deity who is so well known that you can even ask him with help parking the car at the supermarket. As Kierkegaard quipped, if faith would turn water into wine, this turns wine into water.

Or take the speech of the Pope that offended so many Muslims. He argued that Christian theological reasoning reveals the hidden God, because reason – in the second person of the Trinity, the logos – is part of God. To my mind, he forgot the Socratic principle that reason is the key to wisdom not because it shares all understanding, but because it exposes understanding's limits.

And I think this is precisely what Aquinas's silence was about too: it manifests what might be called the agnostic spirit implicit in the religious quest. It is easy to sideline how radically agnostic Aquinas was about God, even as a man of faith. He argued that theology is different from science. In science you know what you are studying (say in physics, the physical world); and its nature and scope (in physics, the universe). However, with theology, you know that it is about God. But the nature and scope of God are entirely unclear.

So, the way all good theology proceeds is by saying what God is not: God is immortal, invisible, unknown. Even the existence of God cannot be asserted, Aquinas thought; and neither God's nonexistence. Such agnosticism is disconcerting. But discarding it turns theology from the pursuit of God into the construction of a deity – that is idolatry.

The agnostic spirit typically irritates atheists too. They say it puts God above reason and so beyond proof. Well, yes. We are talking about God. Take Aquinas 'proofs' of God, one of which is that God is the 'unmoved mover', the source of the movement of all things. The mistake is to presume Aquinas thinks this shows God's existence. He does not. The aim of the proofs is to show how incapable reason is of grasping God. That is its value, to throw us beyond anything that can be said, to God.

Why do this kind of theology? Many philosophers and theologians have testified that the truths of existence are beyond expression. So words about God must be spoken, but ultimately only so a point is reached at which they stop. The final stroke of Aquinas's genius, then, was not crafted by his quill, but was conveyed by his silence.

(Mark Vernon is the author of *Science, Religion and the Meaning of Life* (Palgrave Macmillan, 2006))

**Questions**

1. What reasons does Mark Vernon give in support of the *via negativa*? What does he think are the disadvantages of talking about in God in positive, comprehensible terms?

2. Why does Vernon suggest that an 'agnostic spirit' is to be encouraged?

3. Write a short article in response to this piece: in support of it, or arguing against it, or qualifying it.

# Religious language: symbolic language in the Bible

Look up some examples to see how symbolic language is used in the Bible. Make notes to describe the imagery used, and to say what you think the author is trying to show by using this symbol.

**Some examples from the Old Testament:**

Hosea 11:1–5

Isaiah 64:8

Psalm 23:1

Psalm 93:1

**Some examples from the New Testament**:

John 6:35

John 9:5

1 Corinthians 12:14–26

1 Peter 2:4–8

**For all the passages**

1. Do you think that the symbols are a good way of communicating? Could the same thing have been said more effectively in another way, without symbolic language?

2. Do you think these symbols have stood the test of time – are they as meaningful to us today as they would have been in the historical and cultural context for which they were written?

3. Some people say that using such symbols is too anthropomorphic – it makes us imagine God as a human being, rather than conveying the 'otherness' of God. How far would you agree with this view?

# Religious language: key points revision sheet

- The *via negativa*, or apophatic way, involves speaking about God using only negatives, to avoid making God seem too small. It is supported by thinkers such as Pseudo-Dionysius and Maimonides.

- Aquinas advocated the use of analogy to speak about God, and divided it into analogy of proportion and analogy of attribution.

- Ian Ramsey suggested the use of 'models and qualifiers' to give an indication of God with a reference point in the physical world.

- Myth is suggested as a way of interpreting religious language, but there are difficulties of not knowing when something is meant to be considered a myth. Rudolf. Bultmann proposed demythologising the New Testament, and John Hick edited *The Myth of God Incarnate*, which proposed that language describing Jesus as God incarnate was mythical.

- Paul Tillich and John Macquarrie wrote about the use of symbol in religious language and the ways in which it evokes emotion and existential response as well as conveying meaning through the words.

- The Vienna Circle began discussion of what was meaningful in language, and decided it had to be based on empirical evidence (logical positivism). A. J. Ayer developed this into the verification principle in *Language, Truth and Logic*, and Antony Flew further developed the discussion with his development of the falsification principle in 'Theology and Falsification'. Richard Swinburne, R. M. Hare and R. B. Braithwaite are amongst those who challenge Flew and propose ways in which religious language can be considered to be meaningful.

- Wittgenstein suggested that the meaning of language was best appreciated if we use the idea of 'language games'. Those who participate most fully in the game have the best appreciation of the meaning of the language used, which might be incomprehensible to those who do not 'play the game' at all.

# Religious language: practice exam question

Students' work should be marked in conjunction with Edexcel's levels of response for A2.

**To what extent is Wittgenstein's theory of language games helpful in overcoming the difficulties of religious language?**

## Marking guide

AO1

For AO1, students should aim to give a clear explanation of what the difficulties of religious language might be considered to be. This could include ideas such as the insider/outsider problem of understanding; the difficulties of discerning how something is meant to be interpreted, for example as symbol or myth; the problems of conveying the otherness of God in human terms; the problems raised by verification and falsification. They should also try to explain Wittgenstein's theory of language games and show how it relates to religious language explicitly.

AO2

For high marks in AO2, candidates should try to sustain a line of argument throughout the essay, rather than simply tagging on an unsupported opinion at the end of a long passage of description. When they present the views of different thinkers, they should aim to give some critical comment of those thinkers' views, rather than simply describing them. Outlining a range of different perspectives is description, not evaluation – for high marks in AO2, candidates need to make critical comment by pointing out strengths or weaknesses in different points of view and showing why they are more persuaded by one argument than by another. They should have a clear conclusion. In this essay, they need to assess the language games theory, and also decide whether Wittgenstein's approach solves some, or all, or none of the problems associated with religious language.

# Revision game: match the book with the author

This is a game intended to help students revise the names of various writers and their works, at the end of the course. Copy the following pages onto thin card in two different colours, one for the authors and one for the titles. Cut them up to make sets of cards.

**To play the game**

Mix up the cards and invite students to match the authors with the titles of their books or articles against the clock. If the teaching group is large, duplicate sets could be made and the students put into teams to race against each other. The cards can be used for 'Snap' or 'Pairs' games as well.

As an extension activity, students could be asked to give a brief description of what each book is about and its contribution to the philosophy of religion.

For ease of reference, here is a checklist of the correct authors and titles:

| | |
|---|---|
| Anselm | *Proslogion* |
| A. J. Ayer | *Language, Truth and Logic* |
| Rudolf Bultmann | *New Testament and Mythology* |
| Richard Dawkins | *The God Delusion* |
| Antony Flew | *Theology and Falsification* |
| John Hick | *Death and Eternal Life* |
| William James | *The Varieties of Religious Experience* |
| Keith Ward | *Defending the Soul* |
| J. L. Mackie | *The Miracle of Theism* |
| H. H. Price | *Personal Survival and the Idea of Another World* |
| Ian Stevenson | *Twenty Cases Suggestive of Reincarnation* |
| Richard Swinburne | *Is There a God?* |

| | |
|---|---|
| Anselm | William James |
| A. J. Ayer | Keith Ward |
| Rudolf Bultmann | J. L. Mackie |
| Richard Dawkins | H. H. Price |
| Antony Flew | Ian Stevenson |
| John Hick | Richard Swinburne |

| | |
|---|---|
| *Proslogion* | *The Varieties of Religious Experience* |
| *Language, Truth and Logic* | *Defending the Soul* |
| *New Testament and Mythology* | *The Miracle of Theism* |
| *The God Delusion* | *Personal Survival and the Idea of Another World* |
| *Theology and Falsification* | *Twenty Cases Suggestive of Reincarnation* |
| *Death and Eternal Life* | *Is There a God?* |

# Practice exam questions for Unit 4

**(a) Clarify the argument and/or interpretation in the passage.**

**(b) Do you agree with the idea(s) expressed? Justify your point of view and discuss its implications for understanding religion and human experience.**

Nature constitutes sufficient evidence for the existence of a god. But if the sentence 'God exists' entails no more than that certain types of phenomena occur in certain sequences, then to assert the existence of a god will be simply equivalent to asserting that there is the requisite regularity in nature; and no religious man would admit that this was all he intended to assert in asserting the existence of a god. He would say that in talking about God, he was talking about a transcendent being who might be known through certain empirical manifestations, but certainly could not be defined in terms of those manifestations. But in that case the term 'god' is a metaphysical term. And if 'god' is a metaphysical term, then it cannot be even probable that a god exists. For to say that 'God exists' is to make a metaphysical utterance which cannot be either true or false. And by the same criterion, no sentence which purports to describe the nature of a transcendent god can possess any literal significance.

**(a) Clarify the argument and/or interpretation in the passage.**

**(b) Do you agree with the idea(s) expressed? Justify your point of view and discuss its implications for understanding religion and human experience.**

There are several similarities, Owen suggests, between our intuitive awareness of other people and the believer's intuitive knowledge of God. They can be summed up thus:

(a) Just as a human person reveals their inner nature through their outer acts, so God reveals himself to us in the created order.

(b) Just as there are special moments in which another person's inner self stands out and challenges our attention, so God is known most clearly by his special revelation in Christ.

(c) Just as a human person's acts reveal both their existence as a self and something of their character, so through God's signs in nature and within our experience we learn both of his existence and, to some extent, of his character.

(d) Just as we intuitively grasp that another person is a subject and agent who brings about both physical and spiritual or mental effects, so we apprehend God who creates both material and spiritual realities.

In all these respects, our intuition of the reality of God, like our intuition of other selves, has a 'mediated immediacy'. It is not the product of reasoning or inference, but is none the less mediated by finite things and experiences: in the one case bodily movements, words, behaviour — in the other, general features of the natural world suggesting a divine creator, and particular religiously significant experiences.